MAKING FLEXIBLE ACCESS AND FLEXIBLE SCHEDULING WORK TODAY

MAKING FLEXIBLE ACCESS AND FLEXIBLE SCHEDULING WORK TODAY

Karen Browne Ohlrich

U N L I M I T E D

A Member of the Greenwood Publishing Group

Westport, Connecticut • London

Copyright © 2001 Karen Browne Ohlrich
All Rights Reserved
Printed in the United States of America

No part of this publication may be reproduced, stored in a retrieval system, or transmitted, in any form or by any means, electronic, mechanical, photocopying, recording, or otherwise, without the prior written permission of the publisher.

Libraries Unlimited
88 Post Road West,
Westport, CT 06881
1-800-225-5800
www.lu.com

Library of Congress Cataloging-in-Publication Data

Ohlrich, Karen Browne.
    Making flexible access and flexible scheduling work today / Karen Browne Ohlrich.
        p.cm.
    Includes bibliographical references and index.
    ISBN 1-5608-858-4
    1.   School libraries--United States--Administration. 2. Instructional materials centers--United States--Administration 3. Libraries and students--United States. 4. Schedules, School--United States. I. Title.

Z675.S3 0518 2001
025.1'978--dc21

2001029667

05 04 03 DR 2 3 4 5 6 7 8 9 10

To the school library media specialists
who will provide educational experiences
for our grandson Kyle,
for our future grandchildren,
and for all children

To keep a lamp burning,
we have to keep putting oil in it.
—Mother Teresa

CONTENTS

LIST OF ILLUSTRATIONS

PREFACE

I wrote this book to encourage school library media specialists, school administrators, teachers, and others in the elementary and middle school communities to take a fresh look at utilizing the flexible scheduling of library literacy lessons and at instituting flexible access in their library media centers. Its intent is to put both concepts in the context of the *whole school* educating *whole students* to become lifelong learners, readers, and library users.

In the middle of writing this book, I presented a breakout session on flexible scheduling at the 2000 Colorado Educational Media Association (CEMA) conference. The questions and discussions at that session led me to rethink, reorganize, and rewrite this book. The title and content changed from *Flexible Scheduling, ASAP: A Practical Guide*, a book focused only on flexible scheduling, to *Making Flexible Access and Flexible Scheduling Work Today,* a book focused on two concepts that when implemented in the library media center help our students become what we, as educators, want them to become.

In this book, I stress that the reason for instituting flexible access and for using flexible scheduling is to reach toward a school-wide goal of creating lifelong learners, readers, and library users. "Lifelong learners" have long been mentioned with regard to students and school library media centers; The American Association of School Librarians (1998) *Information Power* continues that focus. I've used the phrase *lifelong learners, readers, and library users,* many, many times in this book to keep me and the reader focused on the purpose for implementing flexible access, flexible scheduling, or both.

It is my hope that readers of this book will go on to become the change agents in their schools, moving them toward a school-wide goal of creating lifelong learners, readers, and library users.

ACKNOWLEDGMENTS

I would like to acknowledge my professional colleagues with whom I have conversed over the years about flexible scheduling and those who have attended my presentations on the subject, often asking excellent questions to challenge my understanding of the concept. A special "thank you" to Betty Morris, who attended one of my sessions and suggested that I write a practical guide about flexible access and flexible scheduling.

Because we do not live near a metropolitan area, I had to rely on interlibrary loans to check the many references I used. My thanks to Barbara Milnor at the Basalt Public Library, Basalt, Colorado, for managing those requests. I also appreciate the following libraries that sent me the majority of background material listed in the bibliography:

Adams State College Library, Alamosa, Colorado

Auraria Library, Denver, Colorado

Baylor University Library, Waco, Texas

Emporia State Library, Emporia, Kansas

Mankato State University, Mankato, Minnesota

Mesa County Valley School District #51, Professional Library, Grand Junction, Colorado

Montana State Library, Helena, Montana

South Dakota State Library, Pierre, South Dakota

Steamboat Junior High School Media Center, Steamboat Springs, Colorado

Three Rivers Library System, Glenwood Springs, Colorado

University of Northern Colorado, Greeley, Colorado

University of Wyoming, Laramie, Wyoming

White Library, Emporia State University, Emporia, Kansas

I am indebted to Jan Adam, Elizabeth Sirimarco Budd, Sharon Coatney, Deborah Cottin, Carmel Huestis, Pamela Getchell, and Debby Mattil at Libraries Unlimited for their help, suggestions, and support. I also thank Laura Dixon, my neighbor, who completed the first edit of my manuscript.

Thanks also to my family and friends who have supported me through this project. Special thanks to my husband, Warren, for his support and for creating the majority of the illustrations.

INTRODUCTION

A flexible schedule versus a fixed schedule for library media lessons began to surface about thirty years ago with the push to integrate library media skills into the classroom curriculum. Articles and books have been written, dissertations justified, presentations made, sessions run, workshops held, directives given, and conversations held regarding how working within a flexible schedule in the school library media center allows a school library media specialist to teach library media lessons in a relevant and timely manner. When library media specialists first began to give library media lessons in a more flexible manner, it didn't take long for them, and for teachers, to see that individual students and small groups also needed to have access to the library media center, its resources, and its services on a flexible basis, giving rise to flexible access. In the past thirty years, flexible scheduling and flexible access have been put into practice at many schools, but others still primarily teach library literacy lessons on a fixed schedule.

As I read and talked about the topic of this book and then began to write about it, I continued to wonder why flexible scheduling is not implemented in every elementary and middle school when it makes such good sense. Many librarians who work within a flexible schedule, including me, say they would never return to a fixed schedule. So why, after some 30 years of existence, is flexible scheduling just a conference topic for many school library media specialists?

The reasons more school library media specialists and schools have not implemented flexible scheduling can be ascertained by perusing the "P" section of the dictionary: *practicality, perception, perplexity, preparation*, and *presentation*.

Many schools see a fixed library media schedule as *practical*. With a fixed library media schedule, school schedules are standardized, teachers have set planning times, administrators know what library media specialists are doing, and their positions are justified because they cover classes. Some library media specialists think it is more practical to stay on a fixed schedule because there are other things happening that need their attention and the support of their administration. A fixed schedule is practical and doesn't upset the "apple cart."

Note: This book provides general information about the setting of school-wide goals, the change process, the integration of skills, the collaboration among staff, and the evaluation of programs as these topics relate to flexible access and flexible scheduling. In this book, the gender of the library media specialist and of students alternate throughout the book to simplify the text.

Rather than offering a vision of flexibility, the *perception* of flexible scheduling may appear to include too many "shoulds." Early descriptions of flexible scheduling and flexible access did have some "shoulds" associated with them. One "should" was that to have flexible scheduling, the whole school needed to integrate library media lessons within thematic units, and that those thematic units had to be on a six-week cycle in which students went to the library media center for six weeks and then did not return for the next six weeks. That "should" raised equity questions with many library media specialists. Another question of equity for students arose with the idea that if a teacher did not make scheduling plans with the library media specialist, then that teacher's class did not have library media lessons. Yet another "should" said that teachers had to stay with their classes during library media lesson time. We tried that "should" at Whiskey Bottom Road Elementary School (Browne and Burton 1989) and found that many of the lessons did not warrant the teacher staying for all library media lessons. I think some library media specialists have heard more "shoulds" than "possibilities," which has hampered the acceptance of the flexible scheduling and access. If a library media specialist perceives that flexible scheduling is more trouble than it's worth, she'll stay with a fixed schedule and meet the students and curriculum needs at one set time each week.

Another reason flexible scheduling and flexible access have not caught on is that changing to this new system is *perplexing*. It is not as easy as simply buying a new set of textbooks, and it is not a linear change. Changing over to flexible scheduling and flexible access involves changes in many areas of the school at once. I know the changeover to flexible scheduling is not linear because I renumbered my chapters at least three or four times as I tried to find the best place to present that particular part of the book's topic. The current Chapter 6 used to be Chapter 3 before it became Chapter 4 and finally Chapter 6 again. Flexible scheduling and flexible access are not always straightforward, and they can be perplexing.

The *preparation* needed to initiate flexible access and flexible scheduling must be taken seriously. Preparing for the change process and for new roles in an old setting is important. Although library media specialists need to be prepared on many fronts, they are not the only ones who will be making changes in the school. Everyone—administrators, staff, students, parents, and the wider school community—are involved in the changeover to implement a school-wide goal. Flexible scheduling and flexible access worked well at Waterloo Elementary School in Columbia, Maryland (Ohlrich 1992) because the school administrators understood the change process and worked with it. Both staff development and total community support are also important preparations as a school implements flexible scheduling and flexible access and work to ensure the success of their implementation.

The *presentation* of flexible scheduling has usually focused on the library media specialist or the library media center, not on the whole school or the total education of the students. Although flexible scheduling and flexible access were said to be the means to an end, they often ended up the *end* rather than the *means*. In this book, I've placed both concepts as a means to creating lifelong learners, readers, and library users. I've delineated between flexible access and flexible scheduling to define each as a concept that can stand by itself. In the school-wide picture of creating lifelong learners, readers, and library users, flexible access to the library media center, its resources, and its services may actually be more valuable than a library literacy lesson. Flexible access is more straightforward to implement and therefore is listed first throughout this book. When flexible access and flexible scheduling are presented simply as something the library media specialist wants to do, their value may be questionable, but when they are presented and implemented as a means to a school-wide goal, their merit increases.

The basic premise of this book is to break down and outline the multiple possibilities connected with flexible access and flexible scheduling so that more schools will be able to implement one or both concepts to help their schools create lifelong learners, readers, and library users. Chapters 1 and 2 give a new *presentation* of flexible access and flexible scheduling, setting both within broader school-wide goals. Chapter 3 discusses the *preparations* a librarian should make before implementing the concepts. Chapter 4 enumerates *practical* ways to partially implement flexible access, scheduling, or both. Chapter 5 continues the discussion to describe fully implementing flexible access and flexible scheduling. Chapter 6 gives a brief outline of the change process in which everyone connected with the school will be involved.

Chapters 7 and 8 consider additional *preparations* that need to be made if a school wants to change the way it teaches its students. Chapter 9 gives the reader a data-driven *perception* of flexible access and flexible scheduling based on current studies and research. The *perplexing* parts of the two concepts are realigned in Chapter 10 with "follow-these-steps" listings.

If the reader is in the midst of implementing *Information Power* and other educational concepts, please take a fresh look at how flexible access and flexible scheduling facilitate and support educational reforms. If the reader's school already has flexible access, flexible scheduling, or both, this book will allow the reader to look at both from another point of view.

This book is also meant to serve as a practical guide for the library media specialist, school administrator, teacher, or school community member. It will break down, show, explain, and then outline the many variables and possibilities connected with flexible access and flexible scheduling. Students have the greatest chance to become lifelong learners, readers, and library users if they are allowed flexible access to the library media center and if their library literacy lessons are relevant and timely.

Be the agent of change in your school for flexible access and flexible scheduling. Create a community of lifelong learners, readers, and library users!

Chapter 1

CREATING LIFELONG LEARNERS, READERS, AND LIBRARY USERS

We, as school library media specialists, educators or other members of a school community who are concerned with students' educational experiences, are privileged to play an important role in a person's journey through the world of learning and reading. We enjoy guiding the questioning, locating, interpreting, inquiring, hypothesizing, planning, problem solving, and criticizing, as well as the management of information, the production of reports, and all the rest of the processes that lead to the creation of lifelong learners, readers, and library users.

Lifelong learners, readers, and library users ask many questions as they move through their lives from childhood, to being students, to adulthood, and to grandparenthood.

Fig. 1.1. A lifelong learner, reader, and library user.

Will you read me this story, daddy?

What's the moon?

Which dinosaur was the biggest?

Where do I find out about the capital of our state and all that other stuff?

Who was Gandhi, what did he do, and what difference did he make in our world?

May I use the video equipment to produce my final report?

When can I check out the sequel?

What were the underlying causes of the World Wars? Are those causes prevalent today?

What do the students in that country think about exploring space? Can I contact them on the Internet?

What do I need to do to get into college, and what colleges should I consider?

How can I get the journal articles I need for this class? What reference can I use to help me with my case study for my law class?

What do the experts say about bringing up babies?

Did you say our company's library has information to help me with my design project?

What did that presidential hopeful state the last time he or she was asked that question?

What resources do you have that might help me with my teenager?

Is it too early for me to look into retirement income?

Do you have his latest book? Can I get it through interlibrary loan?

Should I just log on to the Internet and take a look at the <u>New York Times</u> while I'm here?

Sweet pea, do you want Grammy to read you a story?

CREATING LIFELONG LEARNERS AND EVENTUALLY READERS AND LIBRARY USERS

When children start school, we, as school library media specialists, administrators, educators, or other members of the school community, are presented with our first opportunity to mold the way students meet new information, ideas, and challenges. We encourage them to learn more than what the assignment calls for, to follow their curiosity, and to improve their learning as we assist them in looking for the answers in places beyond textbooks and classrooms. Certainly, we prompt them to use the school library media center and its resources, as well as sources outside the school, to find answers to their questions. The first opportunity for us to develop the desire for lifelong learning in children arises when they start school.

When we create lifelong learners, we use a kind of teaching that is continual, helpful, and encouraging. It's the same kind of teaching that we use with younger children or grandchildren when we teach them to cook, fly a kite, ride a bike, or read a book. It's the kind of teaching that makes a learner feel at ease. It makes them want to continue doing what we taught them, and it makes them eager to find out more, learn more, and do more. This progressive kind of teaching is timely, relevant, and can be put to use immediately. If we want to create lifelong learners, we use a kind of teaching that empowers our students.

If a school community has a goal of creating lifelong learners, it works on that goal every day. Everyone in the school community encourages the attitude of extending a lesson beyond what is required. Questioning, locating, evaluating, inquiring, hypothesizing, criticizing, finding solutions, managing information, producing reports, and all the rest of those processes are reinforced. Open-ended questions are a part of every instructional hour. Higher level questioning and critical-thinking skills are promoted as students learn various strategies that will help them in the future. When students ask questions, mention problems, think critically, and increasingly accept responsibility for their own learning, they are taking steps toward becoming lifelong learners. If a school is to create lifelong learners, it has a full-time job.

The American Association of School Librarians (AASL) and the Association for Educational Communications and Technology (AECT) have issued statements about the library's role in creating lifelong learners in the first sentences of the "Preface" of *Information Power: Building Partnerships for Learning*. It says, "At the end of the second millennium, school library media service has undergone a radical change in emphasis. The focus of school library media programs has moved from resources to students to creating a community of lifelong learners" (American Association of School Librarians and Association for Educational Communications and Technology [AASL/AECT] 1998, p. v. Throughout this book, *Information Power: Building Partnerships for Learning* is cited with permission from the copyright holder. Copyright ©1998 American Library Association and Association for Educational Communications and Technology. Reprinted by permission of the American Library Association).

Information Power goes on to define the goal of a school library media program.

> The goal is to assist all students in becoming active and creative locators, evaluators, and users of information to solve problems and to satisfy their own curiosity. With these abilities, students can become independent, ethical, lifelong learners who achieve personal satisfaction and who contribute responsibly and productively to the learning community and to society as a whole. (AASL/AECT 1998, pp. 2–3)

Individual goals for a school library media program are outlined at length in *Information Power* on pages 6 and 7. Briefly, there are seven goals emphasizing that a library media program should provide intellectual and physical access to information, provide learning experiences for students, and provide leadership, collaboration, and assistance to teachers and others. Furthermore, *Information Power* states that the resources and activities that program provides should contribute to lifelong learning and that learning should allow for diversity. Finally, a library media center must act as an information center of the school. *Information Power* provides a comprehensive outline of the goals for a library media program.

Information Power further outlines the vision of a school library in the second millennium, the standards that students should meet, and ways to build partnerships for learning. The contents of *Information Power* provide a school community with much to ponder and use for their school's benefit.

The AASL has posted many documents on its Web site describing and supporting the library program, information literacy, and other areas of interest to the school community. It has prepared position statements on flexible scheduling, resources-based instruction, the role of the library media program, and other topics. Most recently AASL developed and distributed "The Principal's Manual for Your School Library Media Program" through a grant from the Bound to Stay Bound Books Foundation. The AASL publications provide school library media specialists with a nationally recognized position on the various areas of interest.

In *Harry Potter and the Secret Chamber,* Hermione exclaims, "Harry—I think I've just understood something! I've got to go to the library!" After Hermione's statement, Harry asks his good friend Ron to explain Hermione's behavior to him. Ron responds, "Because that's what Hermione does ... When in doubt, go to the library" (J. K. Rowling, *Harry Potter and the Chamber of Secrets*; New York: Scholastic Press, 1998, p. 255). Hermione not only learns constantly, she also understands that she can find out what she needs to know by using library resources. She uses the library all the time, setting a great example for the many, many readers of the Harry Potter series.

Principal Richard Jordan of Baker Middle School in Denver, Colorado, a Library Power school, says that the library in their school "is the heart and soul of the school. It's both a hangout and a place where kids can come and begin to dream" (Sadowski 1994, p. 35). If a school community wants to be a place where "Hermiones" flourish and the school library is the heart and soul of their school, then they will subscribe to the goal of creating lifelong learners, readers, and library users.

David Loertscher included an illustration in his book *Taxonomies of the School Library Media Program* (Loertscher 1988) that shows how a lifelong library user develops over the years. The illustration shows an acorn in eight stages of its growth into an oak tree that has deep roots in the earth. Loertscher went on to explain that students move incrementally from level one, no involvement with the library media center, through level six, where they come to the library for a lesson. At level seven, the student is self-motivated to use the library media center, and finally at level eight, the student goes on to continue to use libraries after graduating. David Loertscher further stated that the school librarian will "probably never know how many of their students ever achieve this plateau of self-fulfillment. . . . Nevertheless, the goal must be the central focus of all activities—the *raison d'être* of the library media program." After all, the school library program's purpose is to create a foundation for lifelong learning. Teaching students as they grow through eight levels of involvement with the library is the process that develops lifelong learners, readers, and library users.

When we think about creating lifelong learners, it reminds us of the old Chinese proverb, "Give a man a fish, and he will eat for a day. Teach a man to fish, and he will eat for the rest of his life." Or as library media specialists might say, "Give a student a book, and he will have something to read this week. Teach a student to locate, manage, and use the information and materials that he needs, and he will enjoy the lifelong gifts of learning, reading, and using a library."

If a school community chooses to seek the goal of creating lifelong learners, readers, and library users, then it sets about making changes in the school and the library media center. The changes that a school makes might include defining a school-wide or district-wide curriculum, moving to a resource-based curriculum, integrating various curriculums into classroom lessons, and moving toward collaboration among all staff members. A school community might also introduce more technology into the school, hire additional professionals and assistants, or make other general or physical changes in the school. Certainly any changes in a school will be guided by a group of people from the school's community—the school administrators, school library media specialists, key teachers, and others who share an interest in the students' academic and personal growth.

Give a student a book
and he will have something to read this week.
Teach a student to locate, manage, and use
the information and materials he needs
and he will enjoy the lifelong gifts
of learning, reading, and using a library.

Fig. 1.2. A librarian's gift.

If we, as the team guiding the changes in our school, think about what steps we will take to create lifelong learners, readers, and library users, we'd surely want the library media center, its resources, and its services to be available for student and class use whenever they need them. We'd also make sure that classes and groups of students are taught relevant library lessons in a timely manner. In this school, we would simply state that we want every day to be a "library media day," for every day there is the possibility of going to the library media center or having the library media center come to the students. Acting out the goal of creating lifelong learners, readers, and library users would lead us and our school to institute some if not all of the variables of flexible access to the library and to use a flexible schedule for some if not all the library literacy lessons. Changes in how things are done in our school and in the school library media center would have to be made. Making these changes are worth the subsequent results.

INSTITUTING FLEXIBLE ACCESS AS A CATALYST TO CREATE LIFELONG LEARNERS, READERS, AND LIBRARY USERS

If your particular school has instituted or is instituting flexible access to the library media center, then the school community may use it any time during the school day. Students may use it for a variety of reasons. They may brainstorm ideas for a social studies project, look for resources, use e-mail, browse for a pleasure reading book, use a magazine index on CD-ROM, or get assistance from the school library media specialist, library assistants, or volunteers. Having the library media center, its resources, and its services used all day by students, teachers, and other school community members promotes learning.

Jan Buchanan described how her students used the library media center's resources in her book, *Flexible Access Library Media Programs.* She said that one day in the library media center, "As I stepped back from assisting a child and looked around the library media center I realized that each of the fifty or so children in the center at that time had been sent by their teachers for a specific purpose, not because it was the time that the principal has scheduled for them to 'have library.' I had not solicited any of the activity, the teachers had initiated it all" (Buchanan 1991, p. 96). Buchanan told her principal that she was thrilled to see the flexible access program working so well. They had said it would, and it was. With flexible access, students may indeed be in every corner of the library media center all day long, using the library's resources and becoming life-long learners and readers.

If your school has instituted flexible access, students can leave the classroom—individually, in groups, or as a class—when they need to go to the library media center to get what they need. Then they can return to the classroom. Mary D. Lankford, assistant director of Library Services, Texas Education Agency, Austin, Texas, gave an excellent description of how a flexibly accessed library is used in her article, "Flexible Access." She said, "Flexible access helps create students who are excited about learning and are able and eager to complete research projects. Students now design their search strategies in the classroom and use their time on task more efficiently when they arrive in the library. Students dig deeper into information, exceeding the expectations of their teachers. We even heard one second grader say that he needed to return to the library for a better reference book. 'I checked out an information book, and it is *not* a good information book,' he said, 'There is no index!' " (Lankford 1997, p. 11).

It will take this student no more than a few minutes to return the book, look for another, and return to his classroom ready to get to work on the project. This student and many others know where to go to find the resources they need to do their classroom assignments—they need to go to the school library media center. Flexible access allows for individual students, small groups, and classes to come and go from the library media center and use its resources all day long.

If your school has instituted or is instituting flexible access, then the services of the librarian, as listed and explained in Chapter 5 of *Information Power,* "Information Access and Delivery," are readily available.

Information Access and Delivery Principles of School Library Media Programs

Principle 4: The library media program requires flexible and equitable access to information, ideas, and resources for learning.

In a student-centered school library media program, learning needs take precedence over class schedules, school hours, student categorizations, and other logistical concerns. To meet learning needs, the program's resources and services must be available so that information problems can be resolved when they arise. . . . Flexible, equitable, and far-reaching access to the library media program is essential to the development of a vibrant, active learning community (AASL/AECT 1998, p. 89).

The school librarian provides many services to help students and others resolve their information problems. When students are able to "ask the library media specialist" any time during the day, library users are created.

When students are allowed flexible access to the library media center, many visit every day, sometimes even twice a day. Some stop by to check if a book they want has come back; others can't wait to have the library media center as their "center time" when they work independently during their reading time. Other students come with notebooks in hand to use the reference section or the electronic databases. As a school library media specialist, I always enjoyed watching the first graders who had "library" as their center time come into the library media center so quietly. They arrived with a timer in hand and would go straight for their cubbies (bookshelves), the stuffed animals, and the couch. Fifteen minutes later, I'd hear the timer ding and then watch the students put the books and stuffed animals back where they belonged and then leave. I've even seen first graders come in for center time when the library furniture was moved around because I was setting up for a book fair. They were not deterred, but quietly picked out a spot and read until the timer dinged and it was time to return to class. Students with flexible access are not only becoming lifelong learners but also readers and library users.

I also found that I could not turn away a student who was on a quest to find an answer, even if I was on my way out the door. If I said, "I've got to go," the student responded with, "Wait, I'll just be a minute." Of course, there were students who checked out two books a day, returned them the next day, and checked out two more. There were also students who came through the library daily just to see if any Harry Potter, Brian Jacques, or *I Spy* books were in. A time-lapse surveillance film of a library media center with flexible access shows how many lifelong learners, readers, and library users there are in a school. For these student users, a day is not complete without a visit to the library.

Flexible access to the library media center creates an atmosphere in the school that says, "Your quest for knowledge is important to us." Flexible access supports higher level and critical thinking processes. It supports students using many resources, rather than just relying on the teacher or textbook as the primary source of knowledge. It promotes problem solving and communication, rather than memorization of materials and ideas. Flexible access advances the idea that students should learn actively, rather than listen passively to their teachers' lectures. As Ms. Lankford said in her article, "Flexible access is beneficial to the learner. If we want to create an environment to improve student learning, flexible access provides the necessary foundation for improvement. Rigid scheduling of classes into the school library each day or week only serves to destroy a program designed to give students information-gathering skills, an appreciation of literature, and activities to foster lifelong reading and library usage" (Lankford 1994, p. 23).

USING FLEXIBLE SCHEDULING AS A CATALYST TO CREATE LIFELONG LEARNERS, READERS, AND LIBRARY USERS

If you, as a person who shares an interest in students' academic and personal growth, are using or considering the use of a flexible schedule for your school's library literacy lessons, then you may agree that a class or group of students should be scheduled for library literacy lessons based on their curricular learning needs rather than the need to follow a fixed schedule. The length of the lesson time, the frequency of the lessons, and the number of students involved depends on what is being taught and who needs to learn it. The library media specialist may teach the class alone or share the responsibility with the classroom teacher, another staff member, or a school volunteer. The lesson might be held in the classroom or elsewhere.

If your school is using flexible scheduling for library lessons, then the content of such a lesson depends on what the library media specialist, the teacher, the grade-level teachers, or team members have decided it should be. The lesson's content is based on the current classroom curriculum and the information literacy skills that the students should learn and use for this lesson. Information literacy skills are the skills of information problem solving that students and adults need to locate, analyze, evaluate, and communicate information. Through the process of planning for a flexibly scheduled library litcracy lesson, the integration of information literacy skills into the classroom curriculum and the collaboration between the library media specialist and teachers is supported and encouraged. Flexible scheduling increases the likelihood that a library media lesson will provide exactly what the students need to learn.

If your school is using or considering the use of a flexible schedule for the library, you will realize that a flexible schedule provides almost endless possibilities. In just one week, every first-grade class might enter the library media center for a 15-minute introduction to books by their "author of the month." Meanwhile, all the third-grade classes may visit the library twice that week for hour-long lessons during their social studies time when they complete their research and informational postcards about the West Indies islands (see Chapter 7). Also that week, second-grade classes may come for an hour lesson, followed by a half-hour lesson the next week, in conjunction with their urban, suburban, and rural unit (see Chapter 2). That second half-hour lesson can also be taught in the classroom. With flexible scheduling, the appropriate teacher or teachers teach students what they need to know, when they need to know it, for just the right amount of time and the right number of lessons, and these lessons can take place in almost any location at the school or elsewhere.

A student's learning experience is optimized when the flexible scheduling allows for timely and relevant library lessons for the students. Furthermore, as Allison Bernstein, a school library media specialist, noted in her article for *Library Talk,* it is important for students to see and know the connection between their classroom and the library.

> For librarians and teachers the connection between the library and class-room can mean more meaningful use of their time, but for the students the connection can be a lifelong advantage. If students leave elementary school thinking the library is a room unto itself, with little or no connection to the rest of their schooling, this mind-set may follow them throughout their educational careers. Separating the library and its resources from the classroom is a disservice to the library and the children. Children who are brought up seeing the school library as a place to go for informa-tion when it is needed will see the connection in all libraries. If educators see the need for an interdisciplinary approach to curriculum (as do the students), the library media center can then rightly become the informa-tion hub of elementary schools. (Bernstein 1997, p. 11. Reprinted with permission from *Library Talk.* Copyright ©1997 by Linworth Publishing, Inc. All rights reserved.)

The library media center and the library literacy lesson that provides an interdisciplinary approach to the curriculum are best scheduled flexibly, when the students need them.

Although I will share many examples of flexibly scheduled library literacy lessons later in this book, I remember the day that I saw one class twice in a single day. That's what worked best in the schedule, and a flexible schedule permitted this situation to occur. Ms. Welborn's third graders came to the library media center one morning to produce a video that was tied to the New Year's resolutions they had written in language arts class. We made a class video of the students saying their resolutions after reviewing presentation skills with the students. (The tape would later be shown to their parents, but I always kept the tape so it could be spliced into the tape they produced as fifth graders stating what they wanted to do with their lives. The tape also was shown at fifth-grade promotion.) The students were excited about the lesson, a little nervous, yet pleased with the end product. That afternoon, Ms. Welborn brought the students back to the library media center for their second lesson of the day. The students, of course, questioned why they were there again, but we explained that they were there for a lesson that supported their science curriculum. That afternoon, the students used the library's resources for one hour to learn about various inventors. Each student was to return to class with information about an inventor and his or her invention so that the circumstances around the inventions could be compared and contrasted. I fondly remember the look on the students faces that afternoon, and I remember how pleased I was to make the point that they could—and should—see their library literacy lessons as extensions of their classroom lessons. Those students learned that their information literacy skills could be used every day in every class. When those skills are used every day in every class, students learn.

Information Power, in explaining contemporary learning theory, noted that "using the library media center" is the best way to learn.

> Contemporary learning theory describes the student as an active and engaged information user and underscores the importance of the students' developing information expertise. Cognitive psychologists define learning itself as the active building of knowledge through dynamic interaction with information and experience. Theorists in the information field contend that the information search process mirrors this description of the learning process: students actively seek to construct meaning from the sources they encounter and to create products that shape and communicate that meaning effectively. Core elements in both learning and information theory thus converge to suggest that developing expertise in accessing, evaluating, and using information is in fact the authentic learning that modern education seeks to promote. (AASL/AECT 1998, p. 2)

When using the library media center students learn how to locate, access, evaluate, manage, use, and create information resources.

The flexible scheduling of library literacy lessons optimizes the students' learning experiences by facilitating the juxtaposition of the classroom and the library literacy lessons. Having students realize that the library is an extension of their classroom is a service to them. Flexible scheduling promotes the integration of library literacy skills into the classroom curriculum and promotes collaboration among the teachers and library media specialist. Actually, using the library media center is the best way to learn.

HELPING A SCHOOL MOVE TOWARD SCHOOL-WIDE GOALS

Instituting flexible access to the library media center or using flexible scheduling for library literacy lessons also can be used as catalysts to move other areas of a school's program toward educational changes and reforms. If you, as a member of the team seeking to make changes in your school, start by providing more access to the library media center or by flexibly scheduling some library literacy lessons, the rest of the school community will see that providing those opportunities to students really makes a difference in the students' educational experiences. Implementing flexible access, flexible scheduling, or both can be just the catalyst that your school needs to update or reform other aspects of the students' learning experiences.

The Library Power program through the DeWitt Wallace–Reader's Digest Fund awarded grants to various school districts through nonprofit organizations to encourage educational reform through changes in the library media center. Flexible access and flexible scheduling were components of the Library Power program, as was the provision of additional new materials, the renovation of the school library media center, and the provision of a full-time professional library media specialist.

Information Power, which supports flexible access and flexible scheduling, states that

> The primary goal of any school is learning. As effective teaching and learning theory has shifted from a teacher-centered to a student-centered perspective, the school library program has adapted and has become more important than ever in achieving the school's goal. The quality of library media programs is inextricably linked to the quality of education offered in the schools. Schools have evolved to focus on learning, and effective school library media programs have also changed their focus from collections to learning that engages student in pursuing knowledge with and beyond a formal curriculum. A professional school library media specialists is essential to create a dynamic program that challenges students to create personal meaning from information and to participate in a collaborative culture of learning (AASL/AECT 1998, p. 59).

Schools and school library media centers are changing. The Library Power program and *Information Power* agree that what happens in the library media center and how the library media specialist performs her duties play an important role in making educational changes and reforms occur.

A principal at one Library Power school, as quoted in *Lessons from Library Power*, says,

> The old library was not tied to the curriculum in any way. You went to the library to check out a book. Period! Now classes of students, half classes of students, one student, two students, depending upon what is going on in the classroom . . . determines who needs to go. . . . They go in there with their problem . . . that they were trying to find information about. . . . They go right to it. Librarians, parents, volunteers, or assistants, at times are in there to help. In the two years, you almost needed to be here to see the . . . change. But now students have a completely different view of the library. . . . They enjoy going to the library . . . enjoy solving a problem that they . . . can solve in the library. . . . I have seen some of that. 'We are going to the library to see what we can find out. We do not agree on this . . . so we are going to the library.' We still have students who want to check out books, but now they check out books related to some things happening the classroom, almost every time . . . not just some isolated book" (Zweizig and McAfee Hopkins 1999, pp. 49–50. Reprinted by permission from *Lessons from Library Power*. Copyright ©1999 by Libraries Unlimited, Inc. All rights reserved.).

Recent educational changes and reforms ask teachers to team teach, collaborate, and work toward precisely defined student goals and objectives. Teachers are moving toward the use of a variety of resources in varying formats as well as the use of the World Wide Web and Internet to open the doors of the classroom to new educational possibilities. There are many demands placed on teachers to update their skills and teaching style, and these demands need to be met if students' education is to keep up with the ever-changing world. The Library Power program did push the majority of its program schools to use a resource-based curriculum, rather then just text books, to integrate information literacy skills, and to have the school staff's joint planning eventually turn into collaboration. As the school library media centers in the Library Power program underwent reforms, other areas of the school also experienced change. Chapter 9 presents various facts and figures that show how strongly flexible access and flexible scheduling have been supported in the Library Power schools. With the Library Power program, the library and other facets of the students' learning experiences come to life.

If you are also changing the expectations placed on students at your school, flexible access and flexible scheduling allow students to take full advantage of the school library media center and all it has to offer as they now work toward benchmarks and indicators of their proficiency with a subject. Today's students are asked to create portfolios and take performance-based tests to evaluate their progress in a subject rather than just reading a text, taking a multiple choice test, and receiving a static letter grade. Whatever educational changes and reforms are instituted in a school, flexible access and flexible scheduling are working concepts that enhance those changes and reforms.

If you want to hire a full-time professional library media specialist for your school, both Library Power and *Information Power* (AASL/AECT 1998) speak to that issue. Library Power schools were required to employ a full-time, certified library media specialist to participate in the program. Clarence Hoover, district superintendent in the Paterson, New Jersey, schools said, "with or without Library Power, libraries are going to continue to be a central focus of education in Paterson, and the district will continue to have library media specialists." Mr. Hoover went on to say, "It will not go back to the way it was. . . . Libraries will not be treated as the stepchild of the system any more" (Sadowski 1994, p. 33). Once the Paterson, New Jersey, schools had full-time professional library media specialists, renovated library media centers, and a flexible way to teach their students, the difference in the schools was definitely noticed. Library media centers and library media specialists are essential to student learning.

Flexible access to the library media center and flexible scheduling for library literacy lessons serve as catalysts to attain library media center or school-wide goals. Students who have access to library resources and services in their school and who are taught lessons that integrate information literacy skills with what they are learning in the classroom will reap benefits throughout their lives. If you teach students to locate for themselves the information and materials they need, they will enjoy the lifelong gifts of reading, learning, and using the library. Instituting flexible access to the library media center and using flexible scheduling for library literacy lessons will help us work toward the goal of creating lifelong learners, readers, and library users.

Chapter 2

Describing Flexible Access and Flexible Scheduling

The Day School, a hypothetical school, has successfully instituted flexible access in the school's library and utilizes flexible scheduling to teach library lessons.

The Day School's library media center is a busy place. Students, teachers, and community members come into the Day School's library media center for so many reasons every school period. Maybe as many as 40 to 60 percent of the school's population will use the Day School library media center today.

Fig. 2.1. The Day School.

Before the school day starts, the fourth-grade teaching team at the Day School is in the school library media center, looking at resources and making plans with the school library media specialist for the next six weeks. Later, as daily preparations are made, the first bell rings, and students pour into the building. Before the final morning bell rings, 5 to 10 percent of the school's population enters the library to return, check out, or search for materials. A couple of parents also stop in the library media center to check out books to take home for their toddlers. During first period, a sixth-grade class goes to the library media center for a lesson to select appropriate print, nonprint, and electronic resources for their science fair projects. After locating the resources, the second part of the lesson has the students evaluating the resources before they use them. The library media specialist is the lead teacher, and the classroom teacher helps individuals locate materials for the first half of the period. Students who do not finish today will come back tomorrow as a small group to finish. The other sixth-grade classes will come in for the same lessons later in the week. Also during first period, a parent volunteer brings in a reading group to have independent reading in the fiction section, another group of students come in on their own to use the reference section for information to take back to classmates, and a teacher brings in her class to check out books for book reports. The bell rings for second period. The class working with their science project resources stays to continue their work through to the next bell, and soon other students or groups or classes come into the library media center to learn, read, and use its many resources and services.
It's only second period, yet so many have used the library media center.

At the Day School, students use the library media center all day long, teachers bring their students to it to use the resources when they need to, teachers and the librarian make plans together, library media lessons integrate needed skills into the classroom curriculum at the right time, volunteers have an active role in the school, parents check out materials, and the school is student centered. The Day School's library media center is well used, it's supported by the school's administration, and it is greatly appreciated by the school community.

The Day School is making full use of flexible access to the library and has flexible scheduling for all its library literacy lessons. This is the ideal. In reality, a school can institute some flexible access or some flexible scheduling if they cannot fully implement the concepts. A school can also implement one or both of the concepts because one is not dependent on the other. Nonetheless, the two concepts, flexible access and flexible scheduling, do complement each other and logically go together. Any flexible access to the library or the flexible scheduling of library literacy lessons helps create lifelong learners, readers, and library users.

DEFINING FLEXIBLE ACCESS

Because flexible access to the library is a "given" at the Day School, this conversation occurs often; only the names change.

> *Mrs. Collins, may I go to the library? I need to look up some information, return this book, and maybe check out a new book.*
> *Yes, if you can be back in ten minutes.*
> *Can I take Deanna and Paul with me because we're working together?*
> *Yes, but remember to ask an adult for help if you need it so you can be back in ten minutes.*

Flexible access at the Day School allows students, staff, and even community members to use the library media center, its resources, and its services as individuals, small groups, or classes at almost any time a need arises. That's a simple yet sweeping definition. Again, *Information Power's* Principle 4 speaks to this issue: "The library media program requires flexible and equitable access to information, ideas, and resources for learning" (American Association of School Librarians and Association for Educational Communications and Technology [AASL/AECT] 1998, p. 89). *Information Power's* discussion of flexible access continues by outlining how access to the library media program needs to be all inclusive and defining the library media specialist's goals in relation to flexible access. How flexible access functions when it is implemented varies from school to school, but all schools probably have some elements of flexible access in place today.

A definition of flexible access involves three elements. Flexible access allows access to the library media center's space, its resources, and its services.

Flexible Access Allows Access to the Library Media Center's Space

With flexible access, students can easily go to the library media center when necessary. The time frame of their use varies. Flexible access encourages students and others to sit and read, to work at tables, or to be taught a lesson in the library. More than one grade level can be in the library media center at a time. There might even be a class or two, a small group of students from one classroom, and a couple more students from another classroom in the library media center at once. Mary K. Lankford, assistant director of Library Services, Texas Education Agency, Austin, Texas, said, "A library under siege by learners has a higher noise level, is not always in perfect order, and contains some worn out resources. But, such a library is also providing an environment for learning as we have never before witnessed" (Lankford 1994, p. 23). Allowing access to the library media center's space by students, groups, and classes benefits all.

Flexible Access Allows Access to the Resources of the Library Media Center

With flexible access, on any given day, students and others, even class-size groups accompanied by an adult, use the resources of the library media center. Because library media specialists select what is in the collection of a library with great care so that the collection will fill an immediate need or future need, it makes sense to allow students and others to come to the library media center when they need to use the materials. While there, the students might browse the collection; look things up in the catalog; use technology to search databases, periodicals, and the Internet; or use any of the other library resources. More access to the library media center's resources maximizes their use, and soon the library media center does become overrun by learners. *Information Power* (AASL/AECT 1998) even suggests after-hours remote access to the collection. Having access to the library media center's resources twenty-four hours a day, seven days a week, would be an ideal.

Flexible Access Allows Access to the Library Media Center's Services

With flexible access, the services the library media specialist provides are readily available to the learning community. Library media specialists provide many services. They teach lessons, gather resources, evaluate and purchases materials, prepare bibliographies, and track interlibrary loans. These are just a few of the services that library media specialists provide. They can even provide specialized services such as a collection of bilingual books for parents to meet the needs of their school community in addition to the usual services. Having greater knowledge of and access to the services of the library media specialist will help everyone in a school community.

Providing flexible access to the library media center, its resources, and its services transforms a library media center into an extension of the classroom and of the community. The students' learning experiences do not have to stop at the door of the classroom; they continue in the school library media center and even beyond the school walls.

EXPLAINING FLEXIBLE ACCESS

Flexible access, as defined above, allows full and open access to the library media center, its resources, and its services by students, staff, and possibly even community members as individuals, small groups, or classes. Of course, a school community can introduce flexible access gradually in their school or utilize only part of the concept this year and more next year. Chapter 4 outlines how to implement a flexible circulation system as well as how small groups and classes might use the library more flexibly. Chapter 5 outlines other ways to increase access to the school library media center. There are many variables implicit in flexible access to a school library media center, so let's analyze those variables to understand the concept more completely.

First, flexible access allows individuals, small groups, and classes to come into the library media center.

Second, flexible access encourages patrons to come into the school library media center at any time the building is open.

Third, flexible access encourages the library media center to be set up as a self-serve library, allowing the checking out and returning of materials at any time.

Fourth, flexible access allows library media patrons to come into the library media center and check out materials by whatever process can be devised.

Fifth, flexible access highlights the fact that a teacher, assistant, parent volunteer, community volunteer, and even the principal can bring students to the library media center.

Sixth, flexible access suggests that library media patrons can use any part of the library media center that's not in use.

Seventh, flexible access suggests that library media patrons can use any part of the library media center's resources as long as the primary purpose of serving the students is not compromised.

Eighth, flexible access highlights the services offered by the library media center and by the library media specialist.

Fig. 2.2. Characteristics of flexible access.

       First, flexible access allows individuals, small groups, and classes to come into the library media center. Those groups may be made up of students, teachers, staff, volunteers, parents, and other community members. At the Day School, a reading group, a couple of parents, a few students who needed some reference material, plus a whole class looking for book-report books came into the library media center while the library media specialist was teaching a class. Even first graders can work independently in a library media center for independent learning starts when students are given the opportunity to learn independently. Age, ability, or any other grouping should not limit a learner from being allowed to come in. With flexible access, anyone is able to come into the school library media center and use its variety of resources.

       Second, flexible access encourages patrons to come into the school library media center at anytime the building is open. In a flexibly accessed library media center, library media specialists rarely have a quiet moment to themselves because the library media center is providing services to its patrons. Even when it is closed, patrons might enter by remote access. Extending the school library media center's hours to accommodate its users is beneficial to all in the school community.

Third, flexible access encourages the library media center to be set up as a self-serve library, allowing the checking out and returning of materials at any time. Making use of flexible access can negate the necessity of total class checkout on a weekly basis. This fact is a real advantage. Students and others in the school community can check out materials anytime by whatever means is provided. Anyone can check out and return materials when they need to with flexible access.

Fourth, flexible access allows library media patrons to come into the library media center and check out materials by whatever process can be devised. Some schools keep the students' library media cards in rolodexes or picture albums, and others give the students a simple numbers to type into the computer to check out materials; at some schools, students tape their library media cards onto their day planners. At Waterloo Elementary School in Columbia, Maryland, students' library media cards are their hall passes, allowing them to go to the library media center. Whatever system is instituted, it should be well thought out so that it can work smoothly.

Fifth, flexible access highlights the fact that a teacher, assistant, parent volunteer, community volunteer, and even the principal can bring students to the library media center. At the Day School, both a parent and a teacher brought in groups of students to use the library's space and resources. Also other school community members can bring students to the library media center. The group might just drop in, or the person in charge might have signed up for a time in advance. The person in charge of the group might also have checked with the librarian to discuss ways to make their group's visit to the library more worthwhile.

Sixth, flexible access suggests that library media patrons can use any part of the library media center that's not in use. A library is usually larger than a classroom, so it can support more than twenty-five students at any given time. At Waterloo Elementary School, where I was a school library media specialist, the library media center has three main areas. The school's staff decided that any two could be used at a time. Individual students were welcome anytime. Individual students and small groups used the Waterloo library media center often.

Seventh, flexible access suggests that library media patrons can use any of the library media center's resources as long as its primary purpose of serving the students is not compromised. The videos at Waterloo Elementary School were purchased to support the classroom curriculum, and thus it was best to limit their circulation to teachers. We limited the number of holiday books that parents could check out so that teachers would have an ample supply for their classrooms. The primary purpose of the Waterloo Elementary School's library media center was to circulate the materials to classrooms and students. A school library media center can decide on a circulation policy that fits their situation.

Eighth, flexible access highlights the services offered by the library media center and by the library media specialist, who tries to provide as many services as possible for the patrons. The more a service is used, the more it is valued, supported, and even expanded. With flexible access, students and members of the school community have more opportunities to discover and use the services provided by the library media center and the library media specialist. Each school library media center and library media specialist seem to shape the offered services to fit the needs of the community. There are many services that can be offered to the school library media patron.

When a school institutes flexible access, many variables surface. An "all-or-nothing" approach to flexible access isn't necessary. A school can institute as much access as resources allow and then add more access in the future.

DEFINING FLEXIBLE SCHEDULING

With flexible scheduling, a conversation such as the following, between the library media specialist of the Day School and Ms. Bond, the first-grade team leader, is the rule, not the exception.

Mrs. Bond: Let me see. My class will come to the library this afternoon at 1 o'clock for that thirty-minute lesson when we'll introduce our joint autobiography book project. I'll help introduce the project and then let you explain how it will work.

Library Media Specialist: Tomorrow, I'll come over to the classroom just before lunch to take the students' pictures. It will probably take about ten minutes to get them all. Your parent volunteer will be checking in with me on Thursday, and she'll start interviewing the students for their individual pages during your class reading time. Ms. Gershman, your assistant, will get your parent volunteer started because she knows what's involved.

Oh, don't forget, we scheduled another library lesson for Monday but that one's tied into your author-of-the-month program so I'll see your class Monday at 10 o'clock for twenty minutes to introduce Tomie DePaola. Then when I send your students off to physical education, I'll drop a stack of his books off for your classroom library.

It will be great to see your students so often these next two weeks. Thanks for planning with me to make this all happen. I'm sure the autobiography book will be even better this year with the adjustments we've made.

That kind of flexibility with the library media schedule is accepted and expected at the Day School.

With flexible scheduling, instructional time is maximized and used to its best advantage. The example outlined above shows that the first-grade classes will be having many lessons and work times in conjunction with their autobiography project and author-of-the-month program, but those lessons fit around the classroom schedule rather than interrupting it. Flexible scheduling allows a class or group of students to be scheduled for a library lesson at the point-of-need time, to teach, enhance, or reinforce learning experiences using the library media center, its resources, and its services. The lesson could be taught in the classroom or elsewhere. The length and frequency of the lesson and the number of students involved will depend on what needs to be taught and who needs to be learning it. Generally, the lesson is tied to the classroom curriculum and information literacy skills are integrated into the lesson, but not always. Having a flexible schedule does allow for timely and relevant library literacy lessons. The teachers and the library media specialist usually plan together to develop the lessons. The library media specialist usually teaches the lessons, but the classroom teacher or another staff member or community person also may help teach the lesson or be present while the lesson is taught to help the students. With flexible scheduling, the library media specialist's time is focused on meeting the needs of the students and learning community. Flexible scheduling allows for most of the "givens" that are inherent in fixed scheduling to be altered, thereby increasing the possibilities for integrated, collaborative lessons that are timely and relevant to the classroom curriculum and the students' education experiences.

Starting with the basic "givens," flexible scheduling allows library literacy lessons to be held any day, any time, and for any length of time. The lesson can be taught to a whole class, two classes, or a small group; and classes can be held on consecutive days, twice in a week, or whenever. More "givens" can be altered if the class is not taught in the library media center or just by the library media specialist. Flexible scheduling encourages, facilitates, and supports collaborative planning between teachers and the library media specialist. It supports lessons that integrate information literacy skills into the classroom curriculum. This seems like a lot to evaluate, decide, and accomplish, but the teachers and library media specialists in the Irving, Texas, district who switched over to flexible access and scheduling in 1994 said, "Despite the initial apprehension, the lessons we all learned about flexible access (scheduling) over the last school year have turned most of the skeptics into believers. Teachers and librarians who reluctantly accepted the challenge have openly stated that they cannot imagine going back to a rigid schedule. Many librarians have said this was a most difficult year, but also the most rewarding year of their careers" (Lankford 1994, pp. 22–23).

EXPLAINING FLEXIBLE SCHEDULING

Flexible scheduling as defined above allows the appropriate teacher or teachers to instruct students in what they need to know when they need to know it. Any combination of the scheduling variables is good if it fits the needs of the students and their learning. A school may choose to schedule some library literacy lessons flexibly as outlined in Chapter 4 or to schedule almost all of the library literacy lessons flexibly as outlined in Chapter 5. Let's look at the possibilities that flexible scheduling affords through an example of library literacy lessons connected with the second grade's urban, suburban, and rural social studies unit at Waterloo Elementary School.

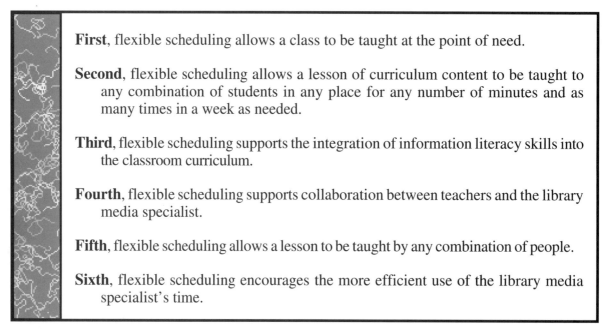

First, flexible scheduling allows a class to be taught at the point of need.

Second, flexible scheduling allows a lesson of curriculum content to be taught to any combination of students in any place for any number of minutes and as many times in a week as needed.

Third, flexible scheduling supports the integration of information literacy skills into the classroom curriculum.

Fourth, flexible scheduling supports collaboration between teachers and the library media specialist.

Fifth, flexible scheduling allows a lesson to be taught by any combination of people.

Sixth, flexible scheduling encourages the more efficient use of the library media specialist's time.

Fig. 2.3. Characteristics of flexible scheduling.

First, flexible scheduling allows a class to be taught at the point of need. If the second grade is studying the urban, suburban, and rural social studies unit in April, the dates of the library lessons are dependent on when the students' maps are completed. (The maps are the basis of the library media part of the lesson.) Since the library literacy lessons are connected with social studies, and second-grade social studies is taught from 2 to 3 p.m., Monday through Thursday, Ms. Charnock, second-grade team leader, organized the unit and made sure that the library literacy lesson times were written in the plan book for the end of April in the 2 to 3 p.m. slots.

Figure 2.4 depicts the schedule for the second-grade library literacy lessons during the last hour of the students' school day. There are four second-grade classes to schedule in the two weeks. Classes 2A and 2B will be finishing their classroom maps first, so they are scheduled at the beginning of the week. Class 2C will move their usual Friday 2 p.m. lesson to Thursday so that they can come in for the library literacy lesson on Friday. Class 2D missed some mapmaking lessons because of their teacher's illness, so they are scheduled in the second week. Planning ahead meant that the second-grade teachers could select the times their classes needed for the project.

Week One	Monday	Tuesday	Wednesday	Thursday	Friday
2 - 2:30	2A	2B			2C
2:30 - 3	2A	2B	2B	2A	2C

Week Two	Monday	Tuesday	Wednesday	Thursday	Friday
2 - 2:30			2D		
2:30 - 3	2C		2D	2D	

Fig. 2.4. Schedule for the urban, suburban, and rural library literacy lessons.

Second, flexible scheduling allows a lesson of curriculum content to be taught to any combination of students in any place for any number of minutes and as many times in a week as needed. There are two lessons with this unit. During the first lesson, the students scale down the three six-foot, group-drawn maps of an urban, suburban, or rural area onto a piece of construction paper. At the end of the first lesson, the students gather to compare and contrast the three different maps each group produced. All groups have used the same symbols and colors. We found that the first lesson takes an hour. The whole class has been working on the unit, so everyone in the class will participate. The second lesson will also have full class participation but can be completed in half an hour. The purpose of the lessons dictates their length. The second lesson includes the making of the atlas by constructing the table of contents, the index, title page, and cover. The two lessons were usually scheduled within two days of each other and taught in the school library media center.

Third, flexible scheduling supports the integration of information literacy skills into the classroom curriculum. This unit covered many skills. Because atlases are standard books in any library, they were explored and the copyright dates of the library's atlases were compared. Table of contents, indexes, compass roses, and map legends were discussed and created, and a computer program was used to create the cover. The classroom skills included mapmaking, elements of maps, and the discussion of the similarities and differences of the places in which we live. A good lesson such as this one can continue to build on the skills that students are using and learning.

Fourth, flexible scheduling supports collaboration between teachers and the library media specialist. The classroom teachers and I planned these lessons during a joint planning time. Ms. Charnock scheduled the planning meeting to fit in everyone's schedule. This was such a successful lesson that it only got better each year we did it. The first year took a lot of planning on our part. The next year, we made a few adjustments in the lesson, so the planning was simplified. The teachers made sure that they made plans with me far enough in advance to insure the success of the lessons, as well as to block out the times that would be needed for the lessons. Planning together only makes a lesson better.

Fifth, flexible scheduling allows a lesson to be taught by any combination of people. Some extra help was needed to have the three student groups work smoothly. The first year the lesson was taught, the teachers stayed with their classes. We found it really hectic for just the teacher and me to work with three map groups, so the next year the grade assistant helped with each class. By the third year, the teachers knew how the lesson was taught and could reinforce the lesson in their classrooms even if they hadn't seen the actual atlas maps being made, so that third year, the grade assistant, a parent volunteer, and I helped the students make the atlas maps. We each took a team. Who is going to teach and who will assist can vary depending on the situation.

Sixth, flexible scheduling encourages more efficient use of the library media specialist's time. Within those two weeks in April, the second graders used the library media center's space, its resources, and its services for one and a half hours. To have the one-hour-long lesson rather than two half-hour lessons meant that materials did not have to be collected and passed out again. To have the two separate lessons almost back to back meant that the flow of the teaching was easy to maintain. These lessons were scheduled and completed with ease. Without flexible scheduling, these lessons would have been taught from 1 to 1:30 p.m. during a fixed library media time over a three-week period, probably in four weeks with spring break interrupting them. Teaching the lessons within a more appropriate time frame increases the students' learning experience.

The second graders' urban, suburban, and rural unit provides a good example of how the "givens" inherent in a fixed schedule are adjusted within a flexible schedule so that students have a stronger educational experience. Many scheduling variables were manipulated for this unit. One of the lessons was an hour and the other a half an hour; the two lessons were usually taught in two days, and three adults guided the students in their projects. Each second-grade atlas, year after year, was a favorite of the students. The skills that they learned stayed with them and were applied to other lessons. Whenever I explained the difference between a table of contents and an index, I used the second-grade atlas as my example. One year, I suggested that we do something else as a culminating event for the unit rather than making those large maps in the classroom; every second-grade teacher vetoed my idea. They wanted to stick with the atlas; it was a favorite of the students.

Being able to teach this two-part library literacy lesson on atlases in just two days because of flexible scheduling added greatly to the students' overall learning experience. The scheduling possibilities are many when library literacy lessons can be flexibly scheduled. In flexibly scheduling library literacy lessons, students realize that learning what they need to know when they need to know it helps them learn even more.

The Day School is creating lifelong learners, readers, and library users with the help of flexible access and flexible scheduling. As flexible access and flexible scheduling have been defined and explained, it is evident that there are many variables that can be adjusted and implemented in numerous ways to match a school's situation. The Day School found the right combination for them.

Chapter 3

MAKING ADJUSTMENTS IN THE LIBRARY MEDIA CENTER

Across town from the Day School is the Night School, another hypothetical school. The Night School is not allowing flexible access to the library media center or using flexible scheduling for library literacy lessons.

If the Night School wants to strive toward the goal of creating lifelong learners, readers, and library users like the Day School in Chapter 2, changes need to be made. After all, the two schools are as different as night and day.

Fig. 3.1. The Night School.

At the Night School, the library media specialist unlocks the library media center door and gets things ready for the day. The electronic card catalog gets turned on, lesson materials are selected for the new fairy-tale unit for the third graders, and the overheads that explain how to use the almanac are gathered for the first-period lesson. When the first-period bells rings, the fourth graders appear. A few almanacs get passed out, and the students are taught how to look up the speed of animals and the longest rivers in the world. Ten minutes before the next bell rings, the students are to look for books to check out. Some students check out books and others do not. The library media specialist sits at the check-out desk and gets the students checked out just before the second-period bell rings. The fourth graders go back to class, and all is quiet.

The Night School library media center is a quiet place—nice and quiet. Twenty-five students have learned something about the almanac and maybe checked out a book. It's only second period. Time to plan a lesson for the second graders.

The Day School is making use of flexible access to the library media center and has flexible scheduling for its library literacy lessons. The Night School does not. It is safe to say that there are many lifelong learners, readers, and library users at the Day School. There may be a few at the Night School as well. The Day School's library media specialist has a sense of his role as it relates to the school attaining its goal of creating lifelong learners. The Night School library media specialist is only thinking about next period. The Day School library media center is supported by the school community and has help with the library's daily tasks. The Night School's library media center does not enjoy these advantages. The Day School library media specialist has a leadership role in the school, and the Night School's does not. The schools are as different as day and night.

If the Night School wants to create lifelong learners, readers, and library users, as well as to raise their students' academic achievement, it needs to get to work. Of course, the Day School didn't just open its doors one day to have all the students flocking to the library media center. Nor were all the library literacy lessons instantly planned collaboratively, with all the necessary skills integrated into them. Those things take time. Bringing about change takes good leaders and a lot of planning.

The process of developing into a Day School library media center means making adjustments in the library media center and in a Night School itself. This process will be advanced and enhanced if the Night School library media specialist adds depth to her role in the school, sets up a library media technology committee, enlists the help of volunteers, and takes steps to assume a leadership role in the school. The library media specialist can institute these four adjustments with guidance and support from the other key people in the school community, especially the administrative team of the school. Having staff development opportunities for the library media specialist that focus on these and other areas of a library media specialist's role reinforces the changes being made. Implementing flexible access and flexible scheduling will go more smoothly and more successfully when the library media specialist is aware of the benefits of these adjustments and follows through with them.

ADDING DEPTH TO THE ROLE OF THE LIBRARY MEDIA SPECIALIST

Teacher, instructional partner, information specialist, and program administrator are the roles for a school library media specialist as outlined in *Information Power* (American Association of School Librarians and Association for Educational Communications and Technology [AASL/AECT] 1998). The latest school library research in Alaska, Pennsylvania, and Colorado gathered by the Library Research Service (Library Research Service [LRS] 2000) delineates many ways that library media specialists in successful schools add depth to these four roles and influence higher academic achievement as measured by state reading test scores in their schools. A brochure titled "How School Librarians Help Kids Achieve Standards: The Second Colorado Study" (Lance, Rodney, Hamilton-Pennell 2000) gives us that information in the percentage of increases in students' reading scores. Those percentages are listed in Chapter 9. Some of the ways library media specialists add depth to their roles are as follows:

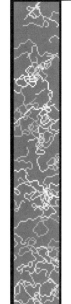

First, library media specialists at successful schools deliver information literacy lessons to the students.

Second, library media specialists plan cooperatively with teachers and share teaching responsibilities when called for at successful schools.

Third, in successful schools, the school community sees the library media specialist as a resource teacher rather than as a "specials" teacher.

Fourth, the library media specialists at successful schools provide in-service training to teachers.

Fifth, library media specialists at schools with higher academic achievement are involved in their own staff development and additional professional courses.

Sixth, library media specialists in successful schools where academic achievement is high are efficient administrators and aware of their patrons needs.

Fig. 3.2. Library media specialists' actions that influence academic achievement.

First, library media specialists at successful schools deliver information literacy lessons to the students. These library media specialists have a direct effect on student achievement because the literacy lessons help students locate, evaluate, assess, manage, and use various resources. When students are better users of information, they will achieve at a higher level. Being an information specialist and teacher enables a library media specialist to teach literacy skills.

Second, library media specialists plan cooperatively with teachers and share teaching responsibilities when that is called for at successful schools. A school that stresses collaboration is a stronger school than one that does not. The fact that the library media specialist is also collaborating with teachers is an added plus. Planning cooperatively with teachers and sharing teaching responsibilities enhances a library media specialist's role as an instructional partner.

Third, in successful schools, the school community sees the library media specialist as a resource teacher rather than as a "specials" teacher. As library media specialists start to make the changeover to flexible access and flexible scheduling, they will want their role to be seen differently than it has been. Library information literacy skills are not stand-alone skills unless a person is a professional library media specialist. The library media center is a resource center, and hence the library media specialist is a resource teacher. Using the library media center often is a step that patrons take when they are learning or enjoying a particular pastime or subject. Information literacy instruction provides students and patrons with the necessary tools to complete their work in the content areas, so library media specialists are not separate from the classroom just as resource teachers are not separate from the classroom. Library media specialists are better aligned with gifted and talented, resource, and reading teachers.

Fourth, the library media specialists at successful schools provide in-service training to teachers. The Alaska and Colorado studies (LRS 2000) point out how important it is for the library media specialist to provide in-service training. Without in-service training, a school's staff become stagnant. With in-service training, a staff continually updates its skills and learns about new resources. "Technology Tuesdays," "Media Mondays," and "Lunch in the Library" are just a few of the promotions that can bring staffs to an in-service. Library media specialists in successful schools assume the role of a staff developer and teacher.

Fifth, library media specialists at schools with higher academic achievement are involved in their own staff development and pursue additional professional courses. They are also active in local and state professional organizations, read professional books and journals, and attend conferences. It is important for library media specialists to go outside their buildings to meet with other library professionals. The Library Power program understands that staff development is a proven tool to help people change the way they approach their responsibilities. In fact, the library media specialists involved with Library Power attended around twenty in-service sessions while participating in the program. Being active in the library profession allows a library media specialist to be in touch with others in the field and to continue to expand one's areas of expertise. Even though being professionally involved takes some additional time and energy, it is such a positive experience that any participation serves one well in the long run. A school benefits by supporting a library media specialist's professional activities.

Sixth, library media specialists in successful schools where academic achievement is high are efficient administrators and aware of their patrons' needs. When library media specialists are efficient, they have time to fulfill all their roles and administer the library media center. When they are aware of their patrons' needs, the patrons use the services of the library media center regularly. Library media specialists at successful schools generally devise policies and procedures that are more user-friendly than institution-friendly. Their policies and procedures are developed with 99 percent of the patrons in mind and allow for the greatest access possible. A user-friendly and efficient library attracts patrons and keeps them coming back.

The Library Research Service (LRS 2000) studies and specifically the Colorado study (Lance, Rodney, Hamilton-Pennell 2000) clearly indicate that when a school has an active professional school library media specialist who fulfills the four roles of teacher, instructional partner, information specialist, and program administrator, one can predict that the students' academic achievement will be higher than it would be otherwise. If the leaders at the Night School want their students to achieve more, they will support their library media specialist as she expands her existing professional roles inside and outside the school.

CREATING A LIBRARY MEDIA TECHNOLOGY COMMITTEE

As a school library media specialist, I avoided having a library media committee for many reasons, although supervisors, conference speakers, and journal articles always told of their strong points. When thirty networked computers first arrived at Waterloo Elementary School (Columbia, Maryland), the members of the Office of Educational Technologies for Howard County Public Schools strongly suggested that we form a technology committee that would include some parent members. Rolling the two committees into one, we formed a library media technology committee. The Waterloo Elementary School Library Media Technology Committee did so much work, was so supportive, and was such a great help to our library media program that I strongly suggest every school institute such a committee.

A library media technology committee allows a library media specialist to gain support from members of the school community. The full name "library media technology committee" is a reminder that the committee oversees three facets of the library media program. It comes to understand, appreciate, and help shape the library program. When forming and working with the library media technology committee, the library media specialist and other key people in a school should be aware of the following:

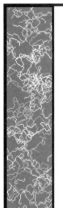

First, the library media technology committee works well if the committee members are library media allies and advocates.

Second, the members of the committee should learn incrementally about the roles and responsibilities of the library and library media specialist.

Third, the committee members can help the library media specialist with many tasks.

Fourth, the committee members' great work needs to be extolled, evaluated, and expanded.

Fig. 3.3. Library media technology committee pointers.

First, the library media technology committee works well if the committee members are library media allies and advocates. Not all committee members have to be teachers. An administrator and a parent or two should also serve on the committee. Our Waterloo Elementary School committee consisted of many grade-level assistants, a few teachers, the assistant principal, and a parent. It would be great to have students on the committee at a middle or high school. Having a variety of supportive members will broaden the commitment to the library media program.

Second, the members of the committee should learn incrementally about the roles and responsibilities of the library media center and library media specialist. Taking part in every decision would overwhelm committee members. Library media specialists juggle four roles and probably just as many budgets. I spent my first year with a committee bringing the committee members on board; I didn't immediately ask for input on budgetary decisions. After the committee members have a better understanding of all the ways the money can be spent, they can offer suggestions and advice during the second year. When working with a library media technology committee, library media specialists should consider dividing information into categories, putting out an agenda beforehand, and other ideas about running a committee.

Third, the committee members can help the library media specialist with many tasks. They can disseminate information to their teams, gather information for the library media specialist from the teams, serve as their team's technology trainer, and emphasize the library media program at grade-level meetings. Committee members are invaluable to the library media specialist when it comes to spreading information about the library media program. They actually become library media representatives in the grade-level team meetings and share information about the library media program when questions are raised in the team area. I trained my committee members in the many new technologies so that they could help their fellow grade-level staff people. I trained eight committee members, then they trained the other forty staff members and were always available to answer any questions. My workload deceased, and the committee members helped me in many ways.

Fourth, the committee members' great work needs to be extolled, evaluated, and expanded. Did I mention we always served food at the meetings? Just a reminder that positive actions also help to maintain a positive approach to committee work, especially if the committee is meeting after school.

Having a library media technology committee is an opportunity to educate many people in the school community about the roles of the library media specialist and to broaden the base of support for the library media program. Having a committee encourages the school community to begin thinking of the library media center as "our" library media center. A library media technology committee is invaluable.

ENLISTING THE HELP OF VOLUNTEERS IN THE LIBRARY MEDIA CENTER

My first library media center parent volunteer was, in all honesty, named Mrs. Necessary. Her son attended our school, Columbia Park Elementary School, in Landover, Maryland. She had always helped in the library media center and politely told me the tasks she was used to doing. Mrs. Necessary is an example of the best kind of volunteer. She always came on the same days, completed her tasks before leaving, and did extra tasks when she had time. While I shelved, she checked in all the books, took care of those that were overdue, and let me know if any were long overdue. However we divided the jobs, I knew that I could count on her to do what she said she would. I've counted on volunteers to complete the majority of the jobs ever since Mrs. Necessary "broke me in" as a volunteer coordinator.

If additional staff is not an option for a busy library media center, volunteers can perform many of the tasks that additional paid staff would. As library media specialists add depth to their roles, they still need to complete the day-to-day tasks. Volunteers are helpful in the Library Power schools. "Two-thirds of the Library Power library media centers use volunteers to perform duties that free the library media specialist to work on tasks more centrally related to curriculum and instruction" (AASL/AECT 1998, 140). To enlist the help of volunteers, the library media specialist needs to *decide, divide, delegate, designate,* and *declare.* Again, clear support from the administrative team of the school and other key leaders will help the library media specialist accomplish these steps when setting up a library volunteer program.

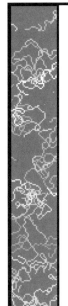

First, a library media specialist has to *decide* individually that someone else can do the daily jobs and then decide which tasks volunteers can handle best.

Second, many library media specialists *divide* tasks among the volunteers based on what they like to do, what training that they have had, and the days and times they can come.

Third, most library media specialists *delegate* a task to specific volunteers that is theirs and theirs alone.

Fourth, a smart library media specialist *designates* a space that is only for the volunteers, providing a desk where they can work, their own office supplies, and a place for their pocketbooks and coats.

Fifth, library media specialists *declare* the volunteers and the volunteer program a success as often as possible.

Fig. 3.4. The volunteers' five "D's".

First, a library media specialist must *decide* individually that someone else can do the daily jobs and then decide which tasks volunteers can best handle. Selecting the books to order, deciding on certain cataloging information, and reading new books are three tasks that the library media specialist should keep, but volunteers can type an order, check in books, put on book jackets, and even type the catalog entry. They can handle jobs that are repetitive and easily categorized and that can be completed sometime within the week, but not immediately. Specific time-related tasks are probably best left to the library media specialist.

A handbook is the most helpful to both volunteers and the library staff. When people do tasks infrequently, a handbook reminds them how to complete all the steps; it is always available to answer questions when the library media specialist is busy with a class. Volunteers are able to do the majority of the daily work as outlined in a handbook.

Second, many library media specialists *divide* tasks among volunteers based on what they like to do, what training that they have had, and the days and times they can come. Some volunteers want to interact with teachers and students, and others are happy working in the back room. Two volunteers may even wish to share tasks.

Figure 3.5 provides an example of a volunteer roster that shows who comes when and what tasks they do. (It is sorted by the day the volunteers come in.) At Waterloo Elementary School, I assigned specific tasks to specific people. When Mrs. Newell said she would be willing to take care of the overdue books but could only come in on Mondays, I scheduled Monday as "overdue day." Mrs. Dresser came Monday morning and cleared every book so that Mrs. Newell could get right to work. Mrs. Justice usually came every week, but sometimes every two weeks. Because her timing was irregular, I put her in charge of the magazines, book repair, and putting on new book jackets. She also changed the posters every month. A grandfather, Mr. Stevens, came in as often as he could. Sometimes he would come in for just half an hour a day; at other times he came for half a day. Because he came in more than once a week, he was a perfect candidate to take charge of audio-visual materials. He even tracked down missing parts and inventoried them for us at the end of the year. Volunteers are happy to accomplish what they can for the library media center.

Phone	Duties	1st	Last	Day - Time		Student
	Ready overdues	H.	Dresser	Mon.	8–12	G.
	Mag., Book repair	M.	Justice	Mon.	10–11	K. & L.
	Overdues	M.	Newell	Mon.	12–3	A. & G.
	New books, Type	J.	Browne	Tues.	8–11	K.
	Everybody's shelves	L.	Dixon	Tues.	12–3	L. & G.
	AV materials	J.	Stevens	Wed.	12–3+	G.
	Bar code problems	A.	Chiang	Wed.	1–3	M.
	Items not found	B.	Stewart	Thurs.	9–11	M. & M.
	Fiction shelves	P.	Newman	Thurs.	10–12	K.
	Non-fiction shelves	N.	Hunt	Thurs.	1–3	N.
	Lab, Teacher stuff	S.	Wang	Fri.	8–10	C.
	New Stu., Catalog entries	B.	Mendez	Fri.	10–1	S.

Fig. 3.5. The volunteer roster.

Third, most library media specialists *delegate* a task to a person that is theirs and theirs alone. Volunteers who are totally responsible for a task will usually get it done as Mr. Stevens did, even if they have to slide into the library media center on another day or after school to complete it. When we were finally able to hire a library media assistant at Waterloo Elementary School (we were pleased to hire Mrs. Newell), she directed the volunteers with any special tasks we needed done, but most had regular tasks to perform. Figure 3.5 lists those jobs that volunteers took on as their own. If there is a parent who can handle complicated tasks, have this parent enter the cataloging; someone else can take charge of stamping the books and putting covers on them. I found that our volunteers called when they could not come and worried about tasks that would be left undone in their absence. Without volunteers, most of the day-to-day tasks would not have been done at Waterloo Elementary School.

Fourth, a smart library media specialist *designates* a space that is only for the volunteers, providing a desk where they can work, for their own office supplies, and for their pocketbooks and coats. The library media center is a great place for parents to hone their secretarial skills, learn to use a computer, or demonstrate punctuality and dependability. I have written many recommendations and been pleased to provide a stepping stone on a volunteer's way to paid employment. At last count, six left their volunteer jobs in the library media center to be employed by Waterloo Elementary School in other capacities. That meant there were six more people on staff who felt the library media center was "our" library media center.

Fifth, library media specialists *declare* the volunteers and the volunteer program a success as often as possible. They evaluate the program as they go along and extend the volunteer program to cover more responsibilities. Sheila Salmon, Elizabeth K. Goldfarb, Melinda Greenblatt, and Anita Phillips Strauss included an excellent chapter in their book, *Power Up Your Library: Creating the New Elementary School Library Program*, called "Support Staff: Filling the Need." The authors outlined not only tasks that paid or volunteer staff can complete, but also ways to recruit and retain volunteers. Their recommendations are helpful and easy to follow.

Enlisting the help of volunteers frees the library media specialist to work on tasks related to teaching, collaborating, scheduling, training, and serving the needs of the library media center's patrons, among other things. For the library media center and the library media specialist to be instrumental in creating lifelong learners, readers, and library users or for them to influence reading test scores, the library media specialist needs be freed from the day-to-day tasks associated with a library media center.

DEVELOPING THE LEADERSHIP ROLE OF THE LIBRARY MEDIA SPECIALIST

If the Night School wishes to become more like the Day School, the library media specialist must develop and assume a leadership role in the school community. That is not always a comfortable role for many library media specialists, but *Information Power* (AASL/AECT 1998) suggests that a library media specialist can work behind the scenes, lead from the middle, or take a more proactive role. This does not mean that a library media specialist must speak at every faculty meeting to be a proactive leader. *Information Power* discusses ways for a library media specialist to show leadership qualities in its Chapter 3, "Collaboration, Leadership, and Technology." The Night School library media specialist needs to develop and assume a leadership role in the school community.

According to Library Research Service's Colorado study, leadership and collaboration go hand in hand (LRS 2000). The study's findings suggest that "classroom teachers are more willing to collaborate with the LMS [library media specialist] if she or he has taken some initiative to become an assertive, involved leader in the school" (LRS 2000). Because schools are more successful if collaboration is evident, it makes sense for a school community to strive toward collaboration and ask their library media specialist to assume a leadership role. The Colorado study (LRS 2000) and the brochure "How School Librarians Help Kids Achieve Standards: The Second Colorado Study" (Lance, Rodney, Hamilton-Pennell 2000) note that at schools where the library media specialist assumes a leadership role and collaborates with the teachers, the library media specialist does many of the following tasks:

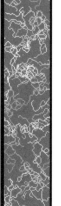

First, library media specialists who are leaders meet with the principal.

Second, library media specialists who assume leadership roles in their school participate in faculty meetings and serve on standards and curriculum committees.

Third, library media specialists who assume a leadership role actively meet with other library media specialists, keep up with the profession, and participate in staff development and professional conferences.

Fourth, library media specialists in leadership roles approach people and challenges in a flexible and positive manner.

Fig. 3.6. Library media specialists' actions that indicate a leadership role.

First, library media specialists who are leaders meet with the principal. Working with the principal effects the integration of information literacy skills into the curriculum and effects collaboration with the teachers. With integration and collaboration, the library media program is stronger and academic achievement is higher. The principal's expectations are important to the success of the library media program and are apt to be more accurate when the library media specialist meets with the principal. Successful library media specialists keep their principals informed.

Second, library media specialists who assume leadership roles in their school participate in faculty meetings and serve on standards and curriculum committees. These library media specialists are leading from the middle and being proactive with their school communities. The Library Power director for Rochester, New York, said the following of the city's library media specialists: "In greater numbers than ever before, library media specialists are sitting in on curriculum and grade-level committees, serving as members of school-based planning teams, and are working with teachers, parent groups, and school administrators to make the library media center a true learning center" (Sadowski 1994, p. 35). Serving on school committees usually places one in a leadership role.

Third, library media specialists who assume a leadership role actively meet with other library media specialists, keep up with the profession, and participate in staff development and professional conferences. (See point 5 in "Adding Depth to the Role of the School Library Media Specialist" earlier in this chapter.)

Fourth, library media specialists in leadership roles approach people and challenges in a flexible and positive manner. Library media specialists emphasize the words "work with," for that's what they do: They work with everyone associated with the school. Library media specialists do not "work at" or "work in spite of" the school community. Working with everyone on the staff is a challenge that becomes a goal.

The Night School library media specialist can work toward being more like the Day School library media specialist and create lifelong learners, readers, and library users by adding depth to her roles as teacher, instructional partner, information specialist, and program administrator. Because instituting flexible access and flexible scheduling will emphasize other areas of the library media program, starting a library media technology committee and a volunteer program will give her the people power to complete necessary tasks and to support the library media program. The Night School library media specialist must develop and assume a leadership role in the school. Being involved in the larger professional community of school library media specialists will give the Night School library media specialist ideas, a sounding board, and support. These are some ways that a library media specialist makes adjustments in the library media center and within her work style that will advance the school's goal of creating lifelong learners, readers, and library users.

Chapter 4

TAKING STEPS FORWARD WITH FLEXIBLE ACCESS AND FLEXIBLE SCHEDULING

The Day School and the Night School are in Anyplace, U.S.A. The Afternoon School is in the next town. The last of our hypothetical schools, it allows some flexible access to the library media center and has a few classes flexibly scheduled for library literacy lessons.

Fig. 4.1. The Afternoon School.

At the Afternoon School, the library media specialist is planning with the fifth-grade team before school about a note-taking lesson that will tie in with their upcoming science unit. When the students enter the building, many of the primary students from across the hall come in to exchange their books. There are just a few from each class. During first period, some first graders are visiting the library media center for their "center" time. The library media specialist greets a second-grade class that is coming in for a third and final segment of a two-week animal research lesson. Later in the classroom, those students will present their research information to each other so that all the students can play the compare-and-contrast game. Part way through the first period, a parent volunteer brings in a reading group of seven for their silent-reading time. They will be in the library media center for only fifteen minutes. First period ends and the library media specialist greets another class.

The Afternoon School library media center is fairly busy. Some students have come into the library media center independently to exchange books, others to read in the library media center; the second-grade class has been in the library media center three times in two weeks. The Afternoon School library media center is doing well.

At the Afternoon School, the library media specialist is taking a step forward to create lifelong learners, readers, and library users. In this hypothetical school example, the library media specialist works with some teachers to encourage the freedom of daily book exchange; plans lessons with other teachers that might meet at "other" times; and integrates information literacy skills into the library literacy lessons. The library media specialist may be doing these independently of any other educational changes going on in the school because she knows that the students will benefit from such a flexible library media program. Then again she may simply be trying the two concepts to see if she wants to suggest that more steps be taken toward fully instituting flexible access and using flexible scheduling (see Chapter 5). Likewise, the school library media specialist, a member of the school's administrative team, a key teacher, or another person interested in the students' academic and personal growth, might have decided to implement the concepts on a limited basis so that there will be a ripple effect out into the school. The changes made in the library media center do push the school community to change the ways they are thinking about students' needs, working with others, and teaching and then other educational changes and reforms will be implemented in the school. If the possibility of becoming an Afternoon School seems realistic to you as a member of a team directing changes in your school, you might want to institute some flexible access to the library media center or use a somewhat flexible schedule for the library literacy lessons. Again, a school can implement one concept without implementing the other, but both concepts do complement each other.

There are many good reasons to proceed with instituting some flexible access and using some flexible scheduling. Let's look at some ways to introduce them together or separately in your school. Flexible access can start with changes in the circulation procedures, by inviting small groups and classes to use the library media center space, or both. Flexible scheduling can start with the teaching of more orientation lessons or with the expansion of a tried-and-true lesson. Library media specialists also can introduce some flexible scheduling by manipulating the library media schedule or adding more classes as the school's schedule changes around holidays and other dates. Taking steps forward—even small steps—to create lifelong learners, readers, and library users is the best direction to go.

INSTITUTING SOME FLEXIBLE ACCESS

At the Afternoon School, primary students come into the library media center to exchange a book, first graders come in for their center time, and small groups or classes use the library media center resources as needed. Flexible access is easily started with the provision of additional checkout times and suggestions that small groups of students use the library media center for curriculum-related projects. Additional checkout times can be announced or may just happen, as was the case at Jeffers Hill Elementary School, Columbia, Maryland. Consider the following, as Mrs. Pat Shrack, library media specialist, addresses a first-grade class:

> *First-grade students, we've had such a great time today locating and reading the books by authors whose last names begin with "S" that I'm afraid all of you might not have time to check out books this afternoon. If you don't get checked out right away, I'll let your teacher know that you can come first thing tomorrow morning.*
>
> *Just to be sure that no one misses out on checking out a book, I'll write down the names of those students who can come in later. Thank you for cooperating and checking out later if you need to.*

Everything went well with the students checking out books later. Most of them came in the next morning. Some of the students who had checked out books the day before also came in. They wanted a new book, and that was fine.

Later that month, an opportunity arose to plan a longer lesson for that same class. The first graders were just starting a unit that could include working on the computer. Mrs. Shrack took that opportunity to have the library literacy lesson with integrated skills go to the end of the period; all the students returned the next morning to check out their books. The teacher agreed with this arrangement and actually preferred it. His classroom was near the library media center, and the students were becoming more independent, so Mrs. Shrack could plan longer lessons and flexible check out for those students. Other first-grade teachers saw what was happening and, one by one, switched to early morning checkout for all their students. Mrs. Shrack is creating lifelong readers.

Flexible access for small groups or classes can start in a similar way. Mrs. Frey, a fifth-grade teacher, asked Mrs. Shrack to gather some books for the next unit. Mrs. Shrack turned the situation around to allow the students the opportunity to use their information and literacy skills. Again, Mrs. Shrack is speaking.

> *Mrs. Frey, because you'd like the students to use some of the science books in the library media center for this next project, how about sending five students down at the beginning of the period, and those students and I can look for the appropriate books. I'll let the students decide which books would be best, teaching them selection and evaluative skills, and then check them out for you. The next time an opportunity to use outside materials comes up, maybe five different students could come. They could use the science reference materials we have on CD-ROM to locate information for the class. I usually don't have a library literacy lesson at this time, so just let me know, and I'll be ready to schedule in a little "mini" information literacy lesson to help them get started.*

Mrs. Frey agreed to the idea and has been sending students to the library media center off and on for additional up-to-date science information. Mrs. Shrack is creating library users.

Soon Mrs. Shrack found that she was busier than before, providing more services to the staff and students. Even with limited flexible access, students and staff began to perceive her and the library media center differently. They began to see that they truly need the library media center each day. Mrs. Shrack is changing Jeffers Hill Elementary School's library media center into an Afternoon School library media center. Her school has some flexible access to the library media center whether they know it or not.

Many schools today already have some form of flexible access. A school community can start with some flexible access and let the concept develop. Many schools have taken steps to implement just flexible book checkout and return, as well as flexible use of the library media space and resources by individuals, small groups, and classes. Let's look at those two aspects of flexible access; the other aspects of flexible access will be discussed in Chapter 5.

Student Checkout Can Be Flexible

Making student checkout flexible is a gift to everyone involved in the school community. Somehow student checkout became tied to the library literacy lesson, and students were allowed to check out books only during their fixed library media time. If students are allowed to check out books at anytime, they will check out more books and lose fewer books. Schools making student checkout and return of materials flexible do so by implementing many of the following steps, if not all of them:

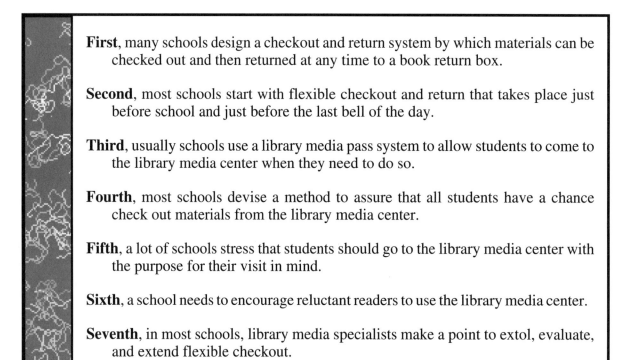

First, many schools design a checkout and return system by which materials can be checked out and then returned at any time to a book return box.

Second, most schools start with flexible checkout and return that takes place just before school and just before the last bell of the day.

Third, usually schools use a library media pass system to allow students to come to the library media center when they need to do so.

Fourth, most schools devise a method to assure that all students have a chance check out materials from the library media center.

Fifth, a lot of schools stress that students should go to the library media center with the purpose for their visit in mind.

Sixth, a school needs to encourage reluctant readers to use the library media center.

Seventh, in most schools, library media specialists make a point to extol, evaluate, and extend flexible checkout.

Fig. 4.2. Steps to make student checkout flexible.

First, many schools design a checkout and return system by which materials can be checked out and returned at any time to a book return box. The library media center at Whiskey Bottom Road Elementary School, Laurel, Maryland, where I was the library media specialist, did not have walls. Hallways were on either side of the library media center. The staff and students came into the library media center at anytime, for there was no way to lock it. Staff was going to use it when they were in the building, and sometimes students even returned a book when they were back in the building for Boy Scouts in the evening. A library media center without walls turned out to be advantageous, encouraging us to create a self-serve system for checking out and returning books.

It is best to design a checkout and return system that is based on the date-due or a barcode on the materials. Organizing checked-out books by date due makes it possible to check in or out any time of day. Organizing book cards by the teacher's names does not. Computerized circulation systems make it even easier to manage circulation. With computerized systems, most schools make the checkout and return system easier, if not self-serve. Computerized systems allow anyone to keep track of who has what. Whichever way the circulation is organized, it needs to be kept simple. Schools with the same circulation system might offer helpful suggestions to each other. It helps to try the system with a couple of grades before using the system school-wide. There are many variables to consider when a self-serve checkout and return system is designed.

If an adult is needed to check out materials then either a volunteer must run the circulation desk during busy times or the library media specialist must step away from a class as needed to help with check out. Most volunteers enjoy the task of checking out books. Books being returned do not need any monitoring. In the end, a self-service system allows the students to come to the library media center anytime during the day to check out and return books, offering more freedom and greater access to the library media center.

Second, most schools start with flexible checkout and return that takes place just before school and just before the last bell of the day. Having checkout and book return during the first and last hour of the day is usually the next step after having them available before and after school. If it is practical, open the library media center for students during their recess. The next step for flexible circulation is to extend flexible checkout and return to all day. If that is not feasible, then the library media center can be open all morning or all afternoon for checkout and return. The amount of time flexible checkout is available can be increased to suit a school community's desires.

It is important to guide the teachers and students into enjoying the possibility of all day checkout and return. Not all teachers are as flexible as Mrs. Collins (Chapter 2) in letting their students go to the library media center any time the need arises. Many teachers designate certain times of the day that are best for the students to be away from classroom activities to visit the library media center, but most usually select the time just before school or before the dismissal bell to have the students go to the library media center. Other good times might include individual reading time, study time, or other times when students are working individually. Teachers can place a poster in the classroom noting the best times to come to the library media center, hence making the students more aware of the possibility of going to the library media center. Having the ability to checkout all day long encourages reading.

Third, usually schools use a pass system to allow students to come to the library media center when they need to do so. At Waterloo Elementary School (Columbia, Maryland), we kept track of who had come to the library media center during the week by moving the student's library media card pass from one pocket to another in the classroom. We labeled the pockets, "Go to the Library Media Center" and "Been to the Library Media Center." Teachers could easily check to see who still needed to visit that week. The student who came to the library media center every day just took their card out of the "Been to the Library media center" pocket and returned. The pockets help keep track of those who haven't been to the library media center. Pockets or check-off lists are additional ways to make sure students have been to the library media center.

Fourth, most schools devise a method to assure that all students have a chance to check out the materials from the library media center. Quite a few of the Library Power schools (Zweizig and McAfee Hopkins 1999) maintained a set checkout time each week for each class, but it was no longer connected to the library literacy lesson time. Some schools had teachers sign up for checkout times. There are teachers that sign up for a monthly book-selection time to coincide with the monthly book report assignment; other teachers prefer to make Monday the library media day for five particular students, Tuesday for five more, and so forth. The a-few-a-day method does provide flexibility for checking out on a daily basis. Total flexibility is not always possible, but any flexibility that can help get students to the library media center is useful. Again, it may be best to allow teachers to start flexible checkout and return to the library media center on a limited basis and build in more flexibility when possible.

Fifth, a lot of schools stress that students should go to the library media center with the purpose for their visit in mind. If students have difficulty focusing when they come to the library media center, suggest that going there is like going to the grocery store. The fact that most people usually go to the store with a grocery list of what they need should suggest to students that they might try that approach to "shopping" in the library media center. Students should come to the library media center knowing what they're looking for. Of course, the display of new books or a friend working at a table might catch one's eye, but at least the students come into the library media center with a purpose in mind.

Sixth, a school needs to encourage reluctant readers to use the library media center. It is important that the library media specialist and other key school community members encourage teachers to plan to let students come to the library media center. They must encourage all students to come to the library media center. There will be students who come to the library media center daily and those who do not come in at all. Library media specialists can form a special leisure-reading group for those who would prefer not to read or perhaps a group for the eager readers who are encouraged to bring a friend. Good books and good reading habits will spread throughout a school community.

Students must check out materials, and there are many ways to make sure this happens. Whatever way you decide to use—passes, pockets, charts, posters, and so forth—you'll want the system to take as little effort to maintain as possible. You'll want a system that gets the students into the library media center to check out books and materials when necessary. You can introduce these ideas gradually.

Seventh, in most schools, library media specialists make a point to extol, evaluate, and extend flexible checkout. It is important to celebrate the fact that students are using the library media center more often with flexible checkout, as well as to recognize and support the teachers who allow their students out of the classroom during the school day.

Even with an informal evaluation, the library media specialist and school community can see what checkout times are busiest and begin to figure out how the program can be extended. Start the program at a comfortable level for the teachers and students. There are many positive "ripples" that go out into a school when students are allowed the opportunity and privilege to check out and return library media materials all day. Designing a circulation system that is self-serve and having teachers encourage students go to the library media center contributes to the creation of lifelong learners, readers, and library users.

Small Groups and Classes Can Use the Library Media Center When Necessary

Allowing flexible access to the library media center's space and its resources by individuals, small groups either independently or with an adult, and by whole classes led by another adult are encouraging the use of the library media center as an annex to the classroom where learning can continue or start. Schools making use of the library media center, its resources, and its services have done so by doing some of the following:

First, schools wishing to attract students to their library media centers rearrange them to accommodate whole classes at a time.

Second, many schools prepare a separate plan book in which teachers can easily sign up to use library media center space.

Third, many library media specialists offer the library media center as a place for students to come during their "center time" when students work independently as a way to introduce flexible access.

Fourth, some library media specialists make it a point to invite small groups into the library media center when appropriate.

Fifth, many library media specialists invite whole classes to use the library media center when it would be helpful.

Sixth, it is important for schools to extol the program's successes, evaluate it, and allow the library media center to be used to capacity.

Fig. 4.3. Steps to take that make the use of the library media center flexible.

First, schools wishing to attract students to their library media centers rearrange them to accommodate two whole classes at a time. The libraries with Library Power grants also renovated their library media space and updated their collections (Zweizig and McAfee Hopkins 1999). If there are at least three designated areas, then two whole classes can be taught at the same time, with the additional space left as a "buffer space." Other seats and tables are located to provide space for individuals and small groups to work. At Waterloo Elementary School, we had three spaces—"nonfiction," "everybody's," and "the reference/central area." If I was teaching in the nonfiction area, someone else was welcome in either of the other areas. A smaller library media center will have a challenge rearranging areas, but the changes will be rewarded with more use of library media center resources. If the resources are available to the students, they will be used, renewed, and maybe a bit worn—but loved.

Second, many schools prepare a separate plan book in which teachers can easily sign up to use library media center space. Individuals and small groups may not have to sign up, but classes should sign up so that the space they want is available for them. Individuals or small groups can adapt and find a work space. Library media specialists fill in the special plan book to indicate the library media center spaces and times they need for the week and then encourage the teachers to come in and sign up for the times and spaces available. If library media specialists work with a flexible schedule, they need to let the teachers know on which day their classes for the next week will be filled in. Having a special plan book to show the use of the library media center such as the one in Figure 4.4 simplifies the process to use the library media center.

The areas of the library media center that the library media specialist needs are crossed out in Figure 4.4. The library media specialist is using everybody's section most of that week. The 2 to 3 p.m. slots indicate that the library media specialist is meeting a class for an hour; it appears that the library literacy lesson will be held in the nonfiction and the reference section at the same time, so another class could not be in the library media center at that time. Small groups and individual students would still be able to find work space in the library media center. Teachers sign up for other spaces by filling in their names. There are plenty of times for teachers to bring in classes throughout the week. As they fill in the special plan book, they might also fill in what they'll be doing to let the library media specialist know. Having a special plan book for library media center-use makes it easy for teachers to see what space is available for their use. Signing up in the plan book guarantees the space they need for their class.

	Monday			Tuesday			Wednesday			Thursday			Friday		
AREA	E	NF	Ref	E	NF	Ref	E	NF	Ref	E	NF	Ref	E	NF	Ref
8:30 - 9					Team Leaders										
9 - 9:30 / 9:30 - 10	✕				↓		✕		✕	✕			✕		
10 - 10:30 / 10:30 - 11	✕														
11 - 11:30 / 11:30 - 12		✕						✕			✕				
12 - 12:30 / 12:30 - 1															
1 - 1:30 / 1:30 - 2		✕			✕			✕							✕
2 - 2:30 / 2:30 - 3	✕				✕	✕	✕	✕			✕	✕		✕	✕
3 - 3:30 / 3:30 - 4							Media Tech Comm Mtg						Bridal Shower		

Fig. 4.4. A plan book that indicates when the library media center is in use.

Third, many library media specialists offer the library media center as a place for students to come during their "center time," when students work independently, as a way to introduce flexible access. This is the reason for the first graders with the timers who were introduced in Chapter 1. Students are encouraged to come to the library media center for leisure reading or to work at "centers" that the library media specialist has created. The library media "centers" are located in study carrels with mazes, old filmstrips, magazine activities, audio tapes, and so forth. The centers are changed monthly and are, hopefully, maintained by a parent volunteer. Students, especially those in primary grades, enjoy being independent and coming to the library media center for center time either alone or with a buddy.

Fourth, some library media specialists make it a point to invite small groups into the library media center when appropriate. Parent volunteers can bring in small groups, or groups of older students can come in on their own. Teachers manage who goes to the library media center to work independently or who goes with someone else. Many of the groups that worked the best at Waterloo Elementary School were small groups sent over with a parent classroom volunteer. These groups used reference materials, read in the "everybody's" section, gathered materials for reports, or used some of the electronic databases. There are lots of reasons to go to the library media center. Sometimes, it just takes a suggestion to the right person for others to use the library media center.

Fifth, many library media specialists invite whole classes to use the library media center when it would be helpful. If one class in a pod or team area wants to have Drop-Everything-And-Read (D.E.A.R.) time when the other classes are working on projects, it is a perfect time to invite the teacher to bring the class into the library media center. Teachers who give monthly book report assignments are invited to the library media center to introduce the particular genre standing right in front of the section where it is found. If a new social studies unit is introduced, the teacher and his class are invited in to use nonfiction and reference resources for any research. With any luck they also search the public library for materials by remote access while they are in the school library media center. Flexible access suggests that teachers bring in their whole class for lessons, using their own materials or those found in the library media center.

Sixth, it is important for schools to extol the program's successes, evaluate it, and allow the library media center to be used to capacity. Students should be able to use the library media center's space and resources at any time.

When a school library media center is rearranged or renovated so that more than one class can be using it at a time, the library media center's space and resources can be used by more than twenty-five students at a time. There are many simple ways to encourage individuals, small groups, and classes to use the library media center independently. Instituting some flexible access makes it possible for the students to check out and return books each day, even if only during a specified hour. Encouraging the use of the library media center's space and its resources by others broadens the knowledge base of the students' learning experiences. Instituting some flexible access in a school library media center is beneficial to the students.

USING SOME FLEXIBLE SCHEDULING

At the Afternoon School, some library literacy lessons are flexibly scheduled in addition to those library literacy lessons taught within a fixed schedule. The Night School has all its library literacy lessons taught within a fixed schedule, so classes come in for their library lessons at the same time each week and that's all. If some flexible scheduling can be worked in around the fixed schedule, additional learning experiences are created for the students.

Figure 4.5 is the curriculum schedule for each grade level. First grade has language arts for the first two hours of the day. Third grade has math and then "specials" and some language arts before they go to lunch and recess. In the afternoon from 1:00 to 2:00 p.m. three grades have social studies, science and health. The other two grades have them from 2:00 to 3:00 p.m. Fifth grade has "specials" first thing in the morning; third grade, second; and so forth, with the first graders having their specials at the end of the day. All of the schedules presented in this book dovetail with this schedule and the "specials" schedule in Figure 4.6.

Figure 4.6 is the "specials" schedule at the Afternoon School. The schedule indicates that there are four classes in each grade level, i.e., 5A, 5B, 5C, and 5D. Every class has music twice

GRADE TIME	1st	2nd	3rd	4th	5th
9 - 9:30 9:30 - 10	LA	LA	Math	LA	Specials
10 - 10:30 10:30 - 11	LA	LA Math	Specials	Math	LA
11 - 11:30 11:30 - 12	Lunch Recess	Math Lunch	LA Lunch	Specials	Math
12 - 12:30 12:30 - 1	Math	Recess LA	Recess LA	Lunch Recess	Lunch Recess
1 - 1:30 1:30 - 2	SS & Sc-H	Specials	LA	SS & Sc-H	SS & Sc-H
2 - 2:30 2:30 - 3	Specials	SS & Sc-H	SS & Sc-H	LA	LA

Fig. 4.5. The curriculum schedule.

a week for half an hour. Art lessons are held once a week for an hour and classes go to physical education lessons three times a week, a half an hour each time. There are two physical education teachers, one is full-time and one is part-time teaching only on Monday mornings, Tuesdays, and Thursdays. The library media center is not listed on this specials schedule because when the library literacy lessons are taught fits around what is being done in the classroom.

No matter what your school's schedules may be, a flexible library media schedule is possible. The following suggestions work with all school schedules. Let's take a look at how introducing some flexible scheduling allows for lessons to be taught at appropriate or near-appropriate times.

	Monday				Tuesday				Wednesday				Thursday				Friday			
	Music	Art	PE-1	PE-2	Music	Art	PE-1	PE-2	Music	Art	PE-1	PE-2	Music	Art	PE-1	PE-2	Music	Art	PE-1	PE-2
9 - 9:30	5B	5C		5A	5D		5C	5A	5B	5A	5C		5C	5D		5A	5A	5B	5C	
9:30 - 10		↓	5D	5B	5C		5D	5B	5D	↓			5A	↓		5B		↓	5D	
10 - 10:30	3A			3B	3A	3C		3B		3B	3C		3D	3A	3C	3B	3B	3D	3C	
10:30 - 11	3C			3D	3B	↓	3A	3D	3D	↓		3A		↓		3D	3C	↓		3A
11 - 11:30	4D		4A	4C	4B	4A		4D	4B	4D	4A		4C	4B	4A	4D	4D	4C		
11:30 - 12	4C		4B			↓	4C		4C	↓		4B	4A		4C		4A	↓		4B
12 - 12:30																				
12:30 - 1																				
1 - 1:30		2C	2B		2A	2D	2B	2C	2C			2D	2D	2A	2B	2C	2D	2B	2C	
1:30 - 2	2A	↓	2D		2B	↓	2A		2B			2A	CHORUS	↓	2D		2C	↓	2A	
2 - 2:30	1B		1A		1D	1A	1C	1B	1A	1B	1C		CHORUS	1D	1C	1B	1A	1C	1B	
2:30 - 3	1C		1D		1C	↓	1D		1D	↓		1A	CHORUS	↓	1A		1B	↓	1D	

Fig. 4.6. The "specials" schedule.

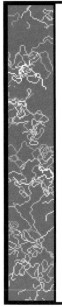

First, more orientation lessons can be taught with flexible scheduling.

Second, library literacy lessons can be expanded and improved when scheduling possibilities are available.

Third, classroom schedules can be adjusted occasionally to accommodate extra library literacy lessons.

Fourth, if the library literacy lessons are taught with the classroom curriculum in mind, then a class might be seen twice in one week or more and the library media lesson might last for an hour rather than thirty minutes.

Fifth, a library media schedule can be fixed one week and flexible the next.

Sixth, with flexible scheduling, fifteen-minute library literacy lessons can be taught.

Fig. 4.7. Ways to use some flexible scheduling.

First, more orientation lessons can be taught with flexible scheduling. Orientation lessons provide a great opportunity to start the year with some flexible scheduling.

Figure 4.8, on page 48, shows the orientation schedule for the first week of school. Schedules are not set in the first few weeks, and it is easy to have classes come into the library media center three times in two weeks. Intermediate classes come in twice the first week and once the second week of school. The primary grades, which are so busy the first week of school, have two orientation lessons the second week of school and one lesson the third week of school.

Figure 4.9, on page 49, shows the orientation schedule for the second week of school. By the third week of school (Figure 5.2, p. 64), when the primary grades are having two orientations, the intermediate classes will be coming in for regular library literacy lessons.

These library literacy lessons fit around the specials' schedule as shown in Figure 4.6. If this plan is followed, most intermediate students will be checking out books the fourth day of school, rather than waiting two weeks to do so. The orientation lessons are not directly connected to any classroom curriculum, but they will be when the first assignment is given or students want something new to read or watch. Three quick orientation lessons, and the library media center is in full swing in two weeks—if not sooner. Orientation lessons get the students excited about using the library media center, its resources, and its services. There is a captive audience in the library media center during orientation lessons. This is when students start to use the library media center for the rest of the year, for the rest of their lives.

Second, library literacy lessons can be expanded and improved when scheduling possibilities are available. The first year, the library literacy lessons around the "Citizenship and National Pride" first-grade social studies unit at Waterloo Elementary School met once a week for two weeks. For this January–February unit, I, as the library media specialist, introduced the biographies of famous people—Martin Luther King Jr., Abraham Lincoln, and George Washington; for the second lesson, I asked students to talk about themselves on an audio tape. The next year, in an effort to make the audio tape portion of the lesson more complete, I asked the first graders to fill out an information sheet about themselves at home with the help of their parents, but the lessons were still scheduled a week apart. The students at Waterloo Elementary School come from many countries, so the idea to have the students produce their own autobiographies came about as the first-grade team and I thought about ways to expand and integrate literacy skills with the social studies unit. If the library media center portion of the unit was expanded to a third week, we were afraid we'd loose the interest of the students and the papers they were to fill out. By the third year, as mentioned in Chapter 2, the unit had expanded to an autobiography unit. The students still learned about the famous people and tape-recorded information about themselves from the sheet we sent home, but we added photographs of the students and asked for information about their birth country's traditions. Now with the questionnaire and the recorded information, the parents who interviewed the students typed up a short autobiography for each student. The library literacy lessons had to spread over three weeks because we needed to make the book cover, title page, and index to complete the project. The classes came to the library media center at least five times in three weeks and worked with the parents all during that time in the classroom. The library literacy lessons became a major part of the unit. We gathered wonderful information from the students about other countries and customs. The project turned out even better because the students' interest was maintained. The first-grade teachers looked forward to this unit, supported the fact that the students were very involved, and rearranged their schedules to fit in everything. The lessons certainly improved and the students clamored to get the autobiography book to read during center time.

Doug Johnson suggested that in approaching the teacher to add more to a previous lesson, the library media specialist might call this "upgrading" last years lesson (Johnson 1999). His idea to upgrade focuses on taking what the teacher is already using and making it better, just as technology upgrades make a computer program better. The library media specialist can start with what the teacher is already doing with a unit, add the upgrade, and create a new configuration to teach last year's lesson. Additionally, Johnson (2000) suggested that rather than starting with the teacher's best lesson, a library media specialist might start with the lesson that the teacher likes the least, perhaps the rock unit. The library media specialist can develop a unit for the teacher, but involve her in the outcome of the unit so she will recognize the results of the library literacy lessons. Together, the teacher and library media specialist can look for new resources and adjust the timeframes of the lessons to better meet the needs of the students the next year. If a unit or lesson is expanded, upgraded, or newly developed, the students learn more because of the extra time and attention put into the lesson.

Third, classroom schedules can be adjusted occasionally to accommodate extra library literacy lessons. It has been my experience over the years that classroom teachers are willing to adjust their schedules for the students' benefit. By looking at the school's schedules, it was plausible that the extra lessons and times would fit into the first-grade schedule. In January and February, the first graders did not have any field trips, testing, or plays scheduled, so when I asked to see the student five times in three weeks, it could be done. The classroom teachers allowed their students to work with the parent typists during their independent center time. Because the teachers allowed the student to work on the project during their reading times, I scheduled the autobiography library literacy lessons to meet back-to-back with their specials rather than taking any social studies time to work on it. Figure 4.6 shows that each first-grade class has three slots during their "specials" time when they are not at a special but could be in the library media center. There were many adjustments made to everyone's schedule, and the lesson was much improved when it was expanded and taught in a three-week period.

	Monday	Tuesday	Wednesday	Thursday	Friday
8 - 8:30 8:30 - 9					
9 - 9:30 9:30 - 10		5B 5A	5D 5C	5B 5C	5D 5A
10 - 10:30 10:30 - 11		3D	3A 3C	3B	3A 3B
11 - 11:30 11:30 - 12		4C 4B	4C 4A	4D	4A
12 - 12:30 12:30 - 1	Lunch			Lunch	Lunch
1 - 1:30 1:30 - 2		Lunch	Lunch		
2 - 2:30 2:30 - 3					
3 - 3:30 3:30 - 4					

Fig. 4.8. Flexibly scheduled orientation lessons, week one.

	Monday	Tuesday	Wednesday	Thursday	Friday
8 - 8:30 8:30 - 9					
9 - 9:30 9:30 - 10		5B 5A	5D 5C		
10 - 10:30 10:30 - 11	3D 3B	3D	3A 3C	3C	
11 - 11:30 11:30 - 12	4B 4D	4C 4B	4A	4D	
12 - 12:30 12:30 - 1	Lunch ————————————————————————————————→				
1 - 1:30 1:30 - 2	2D 2B	2C	2A 2C	2B	2A 2D
2 - 2:30 2:30 - 3	1D 1B	1B	1D 1C	1A 1C	1A
3 - 3:30 3:30 - 4					

Fig. 4.9. Flexibly scheduled orientation lessons, week two.

Fourth, if the library literacy lessons are taught with the classroom curriculum in mind, then a class might be seen twice in one week or more and the library media center lesson might last for an hour rather than thirty minutes. When intermediate grades wish to complete a research unit, the unit does not need to be drawn out over four or more weeks. With some adjustments, the classes can finish their research project in a week.

Figure 4.10 shows that one fifth-grade class works all week on a research project, during their language arts hour time block, with the next class working the next week, and so on. Scheduling the research unit in that manner allows the research questions to be tied into the current classroom curriculum rather than be a student's topic of choice. One class ties their project into their social studies unit, another into their science unit, and another into their current reading book. This way, all classes have done a research unit related to what they are doing in the classroom. Throughout the research project, it is helpful to have the teacher take part in the lesson times to help individual students. This means that the classroom teacher works with the students about forty minutes each day, but still has twenty minutes to plan for his own lessons. The next week another teacher has a lot of planning time. Each teacher has a special week filled with times coming up. Whether the schedule is adjusted or rearranged to fit in extra classes during a week or to fit in a week's worth of classes, the students are taught at the appropriate time in a logical time period.

Week One	Monday	Tuesday	Wednesday	Thursday	Friday
2 - 2:30		5A	5A	5A	5A
2:30 - 3		5A	5A	5A	5A

Week Two	Monday	Tuesday	Wednesday	Thursday	Friday
2 - 2:30	5B	5B	5B		5B
2:30 - 3	5B	5B	5B		5B

Week Three	Monday	Tuesday	Wednesday	Thursday	Friday
2 - 2:30	5C	5C	5C	5C	
2:30 - 3	5C	5C	5C	5C	

Fig. 4.10. Taking one class each week.

Those planning the library media center lesson—teachers and the library media specialist—understand well why the students' library media schedule is going to be different one week, but the students have not taken part in the planning and know only that they're going to the library media center more than once that week. This situation provides an opportunity to reinforce the concept that the library media center is the place to go when they need more information, not just on Tuesdays. When the students have library media lessons more than once a week, they are learning firsthand that the library media center is the first place to go to locate information.

Fifth, a library media schedule can be fixed one week and flexible the next. The authors of *Lessons from Library Power* (Zweizig 1999) note that many library media specialists found that having a fixed/flexible schedule eliminates fears that the classes might miss library media altogether with a flexible schedule. One week, the schedule is fixed; the next it is flexible.

Figure 4.11, on page 52, shows classes coming to the library media center on the fixed schedule back-to-back with their special of the day as shown in Figure 4.6. Figure 4.12, on page 53, shows the same classes having library literacy lessons at times appropriate to the lessons being taught. Figure 4.5 outlines the classroom curriculum schedules that these library media center lesson complement. The third graders are having hour-long lessons for the social studies projects, and the second graders are having joint lessons during language arts time to meet a local author. The fifth grade is having their library literacy lessons during their science time, the first grade during language arts time, and the fourth grade lessons are back-to-back with their specials so that the teachers will have an hour-long planning time on Wednesday. The library media center use schedule in Figure 4.4 reflects this week's library literacy lessons. Another suggestion would be to have two fixed scheduled lessons and two or more flexibly scheduled lessons in the same month. Scheduling either way as long as there is flexibility in the schedule creates a win-win situation for everyone. A compromise that combines the two types of scheduling might convince a school community to completely change over to a flexible schedule.

Sixth, with flexible scheduling, fifteen-minute library literacy lessons can be taught. If the object is to have some flexible scheduling, fifteen-minute lessons go a long way to make the point that the library media center is needed all the time. Who said that a lesson had to be thirty minutes long? Great things can be learned in fifteen minutes or less! A fifteen-minute lesson is like a commercial. The students need to be involved in what is going on and taken to the point of the lesson quickly. Some great fifteen-minute lessons include introducing a new author, genre, unit, or reading story, or giving a lesson that invites students to come in to see where certain materials are held. In some cases, the whole class does not need to come for the lesson; sometimes just a reading group will visit the library media center. Library media specialists can hold the fifteen-minute lessons in the library media center or, better yet, in the classroom. If the majority of the library media center lesson time is spent on a review of how to locate the information, using an index, comparing copyright dates, or practicing note-taking skills, the lesson can be held in the classroom to save time in the students' day. Demonstrating how to use the classroom computer's programs to complete an assignment or a brief introduction of a lesson to be held in the computer lab the next day are other easy lessons to teach in fifteen minutes. It is fun to devise lessons that are taught well in only fifteen minutes. The short lesson is used to make a connection between classroom teachings and library media resources. In or out of the library media center, sharing materials and information does not have to come in thirty-minute blocks.

	Monday	Tuesday	Wednesday	Thursday	Friday
8 - 8:30 8:30 - 9					
9 - 9:30 9:30 - 10	5D Plan	5B 5A	Plan	Plan 5C	Administrative
10 - 10:30 10:30 - 11	KA KB	3D	3A 3C	3B	
11 - 11:30 11:30 - 12	4B 4A	4C 4D	Lunch	Lunch	
12 - 12:30 12:30 - 1	Lunch	Lunch	Plan	Administrative	Lunch
1 - 1:30 1:30 - 2	2B	2C			2A 2D
2 - 2:30 2:30 - 3	KC KD	1B	1D 1C		1A
3 - 3:30 3:30 - 4					

Fig. 4.11. A fixed schedule.

	Monday	Tuesday	Wednesday	Thursday	Friday
8 - 8:30 8:30 - 9					
9 - 9:30 9:30 - 10	1A		2A & B 2C & D	1B 1C	 1D
10 - 10:30 10:30 - 11	KA KB				
11 - 11:30 11:30 - 12	4B		4C 4A	 4D	
12 - 12:30 12:30 - 1					
1 - 1:30 1:30 - 2	 5A	 5B	 5C		 5D
2 - 2:30 2:30 - 3	KC KD	3A 3A	3B 3B	3C 3C	3D 3D
3 - 3:30 3:30 - 4					

Fig. 4.12. A flexible schedule.

Changes in the School's Schedule Can Be Used to the Students' Advantage

A school's schedule has many interruptions in it. There are holidays, testing days, half-days for conferences, and other incidents that turn a five-day week into a three- or four-day week. At the Night School, which has a fixed library media schedule, classes simply miss their library media time in such cases. Library media specialists will find it fairly easy to introduce some flexible scheduling throughout the year around the changes in the school's calendar if they do some preplanning. The school's calendar provides a library media specialist with opportunities to flexibly schedule library literacy lessons in the weeks that do not have five full days of school. Every class can have a library media center lesson when the week is short or students miss school days.

A Short Week Is a Good Thing

Rather than having classes miss library literacy lessons during short weeks, the library media specialist can schedule every class when there is a three- or four-day week.

Figure 4.13 shows that every class can be scheduled in three days without upsetting the rest of the specials' schedule (see Figure 4.6). Here the first-grade library media center lesson will combine two classes. Perhaps these classes are listening to holiday stories or sharing favorite books with each other. Other holiday library literacy lessons can be about finding dinosaur or other favorite nonfiction books at grandmother's hometown library, showing a video explaining magic tricks so the students can wow their relatives, or a lesson demonstrating how to take good pictures and home videos. If the weeks are too short to get all the classes in, then schedule half of the school for library literacy lessons the first shortened week and the second half of the school the next shortened week. With a plan like this, everyone has a library literacy lesson around holiday time, rather than having some students miss their lesson and others getting two. Everyone in the school community will appreciate the fact that classes don't miss library literacy lessons just because there wasn't any school at Thanksgiving time.

Lessons Missed Because of a "Snow Day" (Volcano Day) Are Made Up

When there's a "snow day," teachers don't abandon the lessons that were missed. They squeeze, rearrange, or adjust other classes to fit in the missed lessons. Library media specialists can do the same with missed library media lessons if they are integrated into the classroom curriculum. (The schools in Ecuador, where my friend Ms. Shorey teaches, have "volcano days" when there is too much ash in the sky. They also make up these days at the end of the school year.)

	Monday	Tuesday	Wednesday	Thursday	Friday
8 - 8:30 8:30 - 9					
9 - 9:30 9:30 - 10	5A	5B	5D 5C	THANKSGIVING	THANKSGIVING
10 - 10:30 10:30 - 11	3C 3B	3D	3A		
11 - 11:30 11:30 - 12	4D	4C 4B	4A		
12 - 12:30 12:30 - 1					
1 - 1:30 1:30 - 2	2A 2B	2C	2D		
2 - 2:30 2:30 - 3	1C & 1D 1A & 1B				
3 - 3:30 3:30 - 4					

Fig. 4.13. A flexible schedule around school holidays.

Figure 4.14, on page 56, shows that seven library literacy lessons were missed on Monday because of the snow, and eight library literacy lessons were rescheduled. The class 5B switched their Tuesday library media center lesson to Wednesday so that the kindergarten classes could all come in on Tuesday. If a library literacy lesson cannot be switched to a later time, the classroom teacher could summarize what the lesson was for the students or the library media specialist could incorporate that lesson with the next library literacy lesson. Fitting "snow day" library literacy lessons into a schedule may take extra adjusting, but doing so is worth the trouble.

	Monday	Tuesday	Wednesday	Thursday	Friday
8 - 8:30 8:30 - 9					
9 - 9:30 9:30 - 10	1A		2A & B 2C & D	1B 1C	(1A) 1D
10 - 10:30 10:30 - 11	KA KB	(KA) (KB)			
11 - 11:30 11:30 - 12	4B	(4B)	4C 4A	4D	
12 - 12:30 12:30 - 1					
1 - 1:30 1:30 - 2	5A	(KC) (KD) 5B	5B 5C	(5A)	5D
2 - 2:30 2:30 - 3	KC KD	3A 3A	3B 3B	3C 3C	3D 3D
3 - 3:30 3:30 - 4					

Fig. 4.14. Rescheduling "snow day" classes.

Extra Library Literacy Lessons Can Start Adding Up

If some flexible scheduling is allowed around a school's fixed library media schedule (Figure 4.11), extra library literacy lessons start adding up. When all these suggestions happen, including more orientation lessons, the expansion of various units, adjustments made around shortened weeks or missed school days, students will have at least six additional library literacy lessons a year.

The key to giving each grade level extra library literacy lessons throughout the year is to start planning in August. Figure 4.15 is a listing of the additional library literacy lessons that can be flexibly fit into a fixed schedule. Each grade level has one unit or library literacy lesson upgraded; those units are spread out so the library media specialist and the schedule are not overwhelmed. Holidays and special times in the year provide the other opportunities to add lessons. Each grade level ends up with a 20-percent increase in the number of library literacy lessons taught to their students, with some flexibly scheduled lessons mixed in with the fixed-schedule library literacy lessons. Teachers also end up with additional planning times throughout the year. Using a combination of flexible and fixed schedules, the students have more library literacy lessons during a year.

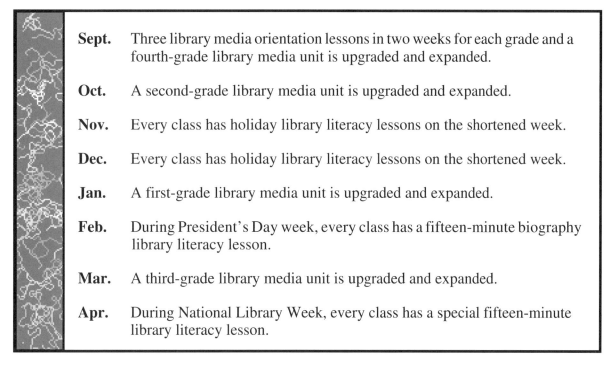

Sept.	Three library media orientation lessons in two weeks for each grade and a fourth-grade library media unit is upgraded and expanded.
Oct.	A second-grade library media unit is upgraded and expanded.
Nov.	Every class has holiday library literacy lessons on the shortened week.
Dec.	Every class has holiday library literacy lessons on the shortened week.
Jan.	A first-grade library media unit is upgraded and expanded.
Feb.	During President's Day week, every class has a fifteen-minute biography library literacy lesson.
Mar.	A third-grade library media unit is upgraded and expanded.
Apr.	During National Library Week, every class has a special fifteen-minute library literacy lesson.

Fig. 4.15. Additional library literacy lessons throughout the year with some flexible scheduling.

When instituting some flexible scheduling as they have at the Afternoon School, the library media specialist reaps the benefits first, the teachers second, and the students a close third. The library media specialist first because her lessons increase in value to both the teachers and students when they are tied to a classroom unit. The teachers benefit because they gain a planning and teaching partner for at least one unit of study, plus they have at least six additional "library media times." The students come in a close third only because it will take a little time for them to realize that the additional library literacy lessons are adding to their educational experiences. There are many reasons to institute flexible scheduling, and they are discussed at greater length in Chapter 9. Flexible scheduling provides more library literacy lessons for students.

The school's administrative team, library media specialist, and other people in the school community may wish to take steps forward to become an Afternoon School by implementing some flexible access and flexible scheduling. If school-wide goals that would change a school into a Day School are not forthcoming, then becoming an Afternoon School will start to create lifelong learners, readers, and library users. If school-wide goals are on their way, becoming an Afternoon School is a chance to learn how flexible access and flexible scheduling can impact a school. Implementing some flexible access and flexible scheduling is better than implementing none. Trying is better than not trying. Creating lifelong learners, readers, and library users is a win-win situation for everyone in the school community.

Chapter 5

BECOMING A DAY SCHOOL

The following is a conversation coming from the Afternoon School's conference room, where the school administrators, library media specialist, and key teachers are talking about their new school goal. All of those involved now consider themselves part of the "change team."

That's what we want. We want to be like the Day School. We want to create lifelong learners, readers, and library users!

Yes, that's our ideal! We want to go beyond being an Afternoon School—we want more! We want to change the way we educate our students.

We want what we're doing to be long lasting and to serve our students after they leave school.

We want our school to be like the Day School!

If you, as a school administrator, library media specialist, educator, or member of the school community, wish to work with others and have your school become a Day School, your school community needs to commit to the school-wide goal of creating lifelong learners, readers, and library users. Certainly your teachers will move from being the "sage on the stage" to the "guide on the side." Becoming a Day School means that your school will be student-centered and that the students' learning experiences will be active, timely, and relevant. There will be many changes to make in the school, as well as in the library media center. If your school wishes to be like the Day School, it will move toward and accomplish the following in the next few years: establishing a resource-based curriculum, integrating skills, and creating collaboration among all staff members. Lastly, if your school becomes a Day School, flexible access will be fully instituted and flexible scheduling will be fully used to help your school reach the goal of creating lifelong learners, readers, and library users.

FULLY INSTITUTING FLEXIBLE ACCESS

To fully institute flexible access means that your library media center, its resources, and its services are available to everyone in the school community for as much time as possible, twenty-four hours a day, seven days a week. The basic premise of flexible access, the steps to take to ensure that students can check out materials during the school hours, and the ways to encourage individuals, groups, and classes to use the library media center were discussed in Chapters 2 and 4. The steps outlined here point to ways in which access to the school library media center can be widened even more. The implementation of these steps can be adapted for any school. The idea is to make the school library media center as accessible as possible to the school community.

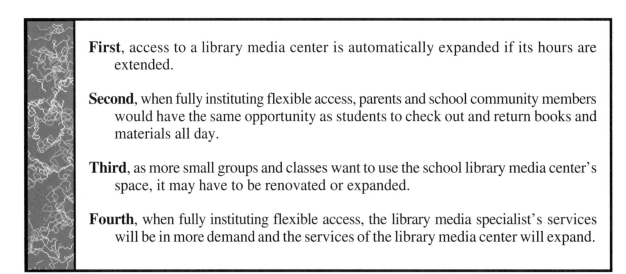

First, access to a library media center is automatically expanded if its hours are extended.

Second, when fully instituting flexible access, parents and school community members would have the same opportunity as students to check out and return books and materials all day.

Third, as more small groups and classes want to use the school library media center's space, it may have to be renovated or expanded.

Fourth, when fully instituting flexible access, the library media specialist's services will be in more demand and the services of the library media center will expand.

Fig. 5.1. Steps to expand flexible access.

First, access to a library media center is automatically expanded if its hours are extended. It is helpful to look at the school community's use patterns before deciding how to extend the library media center's hours. If a lot of students come to school early or remain in the building after the last bell, extending the hours of operation of the school library media center is an excellent idea. If all the students arrive and go home on buses, there isn't a reason to extend hours; but if there isn't a public library media center nearby, it could make sense to open the school library media center to the community at hours different from school hours. It may also make sense to have the library media center open during the summer if the students will not have access to other library books during that time. Additional staffing for the library media center or the utilization of more volunteers may be necessary if the school decides to extend the hours or days of operation. Such a decision should be based on the needs of the learning community. Usually any extension of the hours of operation is welcome. Allowing the circulation of materials at any time is quite possible and creates open access to the library media center, encouraging students and members of the school community to become readers.

Second, when fully instituting flexible access, parents and school community members would have the same opportunity as students to check out and return books and materials all day. Extending the library media center patron list to include parents and school community members is always well received. We offered this opportunity to the parents of the students at Waterloo Elementary School in Columbia, Maryland, because the three public libraries that serve the school community are out of the normal driving patterns of the school families. Once there was computerized circulation at Waterloo Elementary School, it was easy to allow the parents to check out books. Library media card applications were filled out at the first Parents Teachers Association meeting, and we gave out library media cards the first time they came to the library media center. The program was successful, especially for those mothers who had little ones at home or drove their students to school most days. The school's circulation figures jumped, and the number of overdue books did not. The public relations generated by the extending of the patron list was worthwhile.

Information Power (American Association of School Librarians and Association for Educational Communications and Technology [AASL/AECT] 1998) strongly suggests that the school library media center should be a community library media center. The wider community should be able to use its resources as long as their use does not interrupt the library media center's primary purpose—to serve the students. With the access to the library media center, its recourses, and its services extended to parents and members of the school community, a broader base of support for the library media center, the school's administration, and the school will be rallied. These changes may necessitate funding for new technology to allow remote access, but having the library media center open all the time will generate parental and community support. More parental and community support for the library media center means a better library media program and school. Now everyone—students and school community members—will be able to become lifelong learners.

Third, as more small groups and classes want to use the library media center's space, it may have to be renovated or expanded. The school will need to locate funding for those projects, and perhaps for the purchase of new materials to draw students and teachers into the library media center. Having more comfortable and attractive space available for use in the library media center at any time will certainly help create library users.

Fourth, when fully instituting flexible access, the school library media specialist's services will be in more demand and the services of the library media center will expand. Again, this change may necessitate the utilization of more volunteers or the hiring of additional staff. Almost every successful business has had to expand and add more staff to meet the demands of their customers.

The same will happen in the school library media center when the patrons' needs are met. Providing many services to the school library media center patrons will make them library users. With administrative support and some additional funding, full access to the school library media center can be accomplished. As logistics are worked out, students, teachers, and members of the school's community will see the library media center as an extension of the classroom. A school library media center can be filled to capacity every hour, just like the Day School library media center. What a great use of resources! What a great way to create lifelong learners, readers, and library users!

FULLY UTILIZING FLEXIBLE SCHEDULING

When fully utilizing flexible scheduling, a school library media specialist's plan book starts out blank—nothing is scheduled. Classes are then scheduled when the library literacy lessons are timely and relevant. At the Day School, the library media specialist looks in his plan book. It's the third week of school, orientation lessons are winding down, and the plan book is essentially blank.

The plan book was blank. The second-grade team leader asked if the Day School library media specialist could teach the students about writing poetry to integrate with their unit on undersea animals. Next, the fourth-grade teachers ask his help with their Native American unit. They want the students to create a database using information about all the tribes after the class has had two days to research the data in the library media center.

His plan book is getting filled in.

Later in the day, the third-grade team asks if the library media specialist could help each class write their own Japanese folktale at the conclusion of their social studies unit on Japan. Before the Day School library media specialist goes home, the principal lets him know there is extra money in the school's budget if it can be spent in the next two weeks!

More time is filled in.

The next day, the fifth-grade team asks him to plan with them on Tuesday to decide which information literacy skills can be integrated into the science curriculum.

More times are filled in.

Next a first-grade teacher asks if her reading group could come over tomorrow to learn more about bears.

The library media specialist quickly fills in his lunch and planning time before all the slots are taken. He must also fill in the library media center technology committee meeting on Tuesday.

Any of these activities can take from fifteen minutes to a few hours or a few classes over the following two or three weeks. Figure 5.2, on page 64, shows that the library media specialist has allowed the lessons and himself appropriate amounts of time, although he will have to eat lunch on Thursday and Friday while he reads reviews to decide where he wants to spend money. His afternoons are busy with orientation lessons and the fourth- and third-grade units will start at the end of the week.

Figure 5.3, on page 65, is the fourth week of school. By Monday at lunchtime, the library media specialist will have the money spent and the fourth- and third-grade units continue. This week, the fourth graders will spend an hour in the library media center doing their research after their introductory lesson. Next week, they'll finish their research and start working in the computer lab.

The third graders will start this week with a half-hour lesson to review folktales and "meet" a Japanese folktale. In the next lesson, the class will hear another Japanese folktale, look for other information about Japan, and outline what they need to learn to have enough material to create their own folktale. The second-grade poetry unit will start on Wednesday and continue into week five. Each activity is a request from a teacher for lessons, materials, or services. Various members of the school's staff have also requested administrative and planning time. All these activities and lessons create a full—albeit flexible—schedule. The Day School library media specialist has learned to balance, realign, and adjust the library media schedule to meet as many needs as possible. Any other school that wants to use flexible scheduling will have to learn to do the same. Yes, a flexible schedule starts out blank, but it fills up fast.

A Library Media Specialist's Plan Book Can Fill Up Fast

If you and others at your school want to create lifelong learners, readers, and library users, your students will be given relevant library literacy lessons at the point of need. How can all students receive their lessons at the right time? To understand how a schedule can be flexible and yet meet everyone's needs, think of how you schedule your weekends. There are both small and large slots of time to schedule. You may need only the time it takes to clean the yard or a whole weekend for a yard sale. Perhaps a short walk after dinner would be a nice break, or maybe you have scheduled a weekend getaway. For many, children's activities greatly influence a weekend schedule, but the necessary tasks, such as shopping and cleaning, still seem to get done. It is safe to say that no two weekends are alike, just as no two school days are alike in a school library media center with flexible scheduling. What needs to get done gets done. The library media specialist usually can fit most things in or realign something so that things are accomplished. One thing is for sure, the weekend calendar or the blank plan book fills up fast.

The basic premise of flexible scheduling, and ways to implement some flexible scheduling in a school around orientation lessons, a great lesson, fifteen-minute lessons, and school schedule changes are discussed in Chapters 2 and 4. The following on page 66 are some of the possibilities when a school fully uses a flexible schedule.

	Monday	Tuesday	Wednesday	Thursday	Friday
8 - 8:30 8:30 - 9					
9 - 9:30 9:30 - 10		Admin Time		Plan Media Tech Mtg	2D 2C
10 - 10:30 10:30 - 11		1A - Bears			
11 - 11:30 11:30 - 12	Lunch		Plan 3rd	Spend	Money
12 - 12:30 12:30 - 1		Lunch	Lunch	Spend	Money
1 - 1:30 1:30 - 2	2D - Orient. 2B - Orient.	2C - Orient.	2A - Orient.		4C 4D
2 - 2:30 2:30 - 3	1C - Orient. 1A - Orient.	1B - Orient.	1D - Orient.		3C 3D
3 - 3:30 3:30 - 4				Pass out Media Tech Agenda	

Fig. 5.2. A flexibly scheduled plan book, week three.

	Monday	Tuesday	Wednesday	Thursday	Friday
8 - 8:30 8:30 - 9	Spend Money				
9 - 9:30 9:30 - 10		Plan 5th	2A 2B	2D 2C	2A 2B
10 - 10:30 10:30 - 11		Gather for Media			
11 - 11:30 11:30 - 12		Tech Meeting	Lunch	Lunch	Lunch
12 - 12:30 12:30 - 1	Lunch	Lunch	Plan	Plan	Plan
1 - 1:30 1:30 - 2	4A 4B	4A 4A	4B 4B	4C 4C	4D 4D
2 - 2:30 2:30 - 3	3A 3B	3B 3B	3C 3C	3D 3D	3A 3A
3 - 3:30 3:30 - 4		Media Tech Meeting			

Fig. 5.3. A flexibly scheduled plan book, week four.

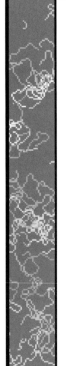

First, the library media schedule is to be flexible so that it fits the needs of the school.

Second, the school's schedules always come first, but that's okay.

Third, a school library media specialist's schedule still has a lot of flexibility around the other schedules.

Fourth, sometimes a library literacy lesson is best taught back-to-back with a class' special so that the teacher or team can have a longer planning time to accomplish tasks such as report cards, conferences, or field trip preparation.

Fifth, integrated library literacy lessons can fit into a schedule as closely as possible to the curriculum time if it can't be taught during the curriculum time.

Sixth, often the library literacy lessons that are integrated with a curriculum unit can be covered in a few weeks' time.

Seventh, if a school wants all library literacy lessons to be integrated and taught in conjunction with a long curriculum unit, that also can be done.

Eighth, with a flexible schedule, the library media center can accommodate almost any school-wide classroom scheduling scheme.

Fig. 5.4. Possibilities with flexible scheduling.

First, the library media schedule is to be flexible so that it fits the needs of the school. The Library Power program mandated that the schools involved with the program would have flexible access and scheduling. Seventy-five percent of the schools were in fact fully flexible. Twenty percent developed a schedule that was a mix of a flexible and a fixed schedule. Five percent of the schools maintained a fixed schedule. The authors of *Lessons from Library Power* stated that flexible access and scheduling "was implemented in a variety of patterns and with varying effects on use of the library. . . . Librarians, teachers, and principals have made adaptations to help flexible scheduling work for their schools" (Zweizig and McAfee Hopkins 1999, p. 39). The main idea is to have the library media schedule fit the needs of the classroom curriculum and the learning experiences of the students. A flexible schedule can always fit the needs of the school.

Second, the school's schedules always come first, but that's okay. A school plans how its day will be scheduled, how long the "specials" (art, physical education, music) will be, who goes to lunch and recess at given times, and in what order the grades will go to their specials. Figure 4.6 is the Afternoon School's specials schedule. The specials schedule takes into account the adaptability of the students so that the first graders go to specials during the last period and the fifth graders go first thing in the morning. One hopes to schedule a special for each class each day. If possible, it would be best if all the students in one grade could attend specials for at least an hour once a week. The specials schedule should support the teacher's as well as the students' needs.

Each grade or classroom has a curriculum schedule that indicates when language arts, science, social studies, and other subjects are taught. Figure 4.5 is the curriculum schedule for the Afternoon School. The classroom schedule takes into account not only when the students will be fresh enough to learn the basic subjects but also the schedules of the language arts and math resource teachers. One can see in the curriculum schedule shown in Figure 4.5 that the language arts resource teacher can work with all grades in one day. Math classes are also spread throughout the day. Most social studies and science classes are held in the afternoon. If every grade wants to combine their social studies and science lessons with the library media center, there will be a bottleneck in the 1:00 to 2:00 p.m. and the 2:00 to 3:00 p.m. time slots, but remember that the schedule is flexible. Other factors that enter into the schedule picture are the band schedule, the pullout program schedules, and so forth. The library media center schedule fits in and around all of those schedules when it's fixed or when it's flexible. Even though there are limits on the flexibility of the library media schedule because of other schedules, some flexibility is so much better than none.

	Monday	Tuesday	Wednesday	Thursday	Friday
8 - 8:30 8:30 - 9	Presidents' Day		Team Leaders	Tech Lesson	
9 - 9:30 9:30 - 10		Admin Time		Parent Volunteer Training	
10 - 10:30 10:30 - 11		KA KB		5B 5C	5D 5A
11 - 11:30 11:30 - 12		Lunch Plan	4C 4A	Principal mtg. (budget) Plan 1st	4B 4D
12 - 12:30 12:30 - 1		Parent Volunteers	Lunch Plan	Team mtg. Lunch	Lunch Lunch
1 - 1:30 1:30 - 2		KC KD	Plan 2C	Plan 2B	2A 2D
2 - 2:30 2:30 - 3		3D 3D	3A 3A	3B 3B	3C 3C
3 - 3:30 3:30 - 4		Budget Plan 4th	Faculty Meeting	Book Fair Preview	

Fig. 5.5. A flexibly scheduled week.

Third, a school library media specialist's schedule still has a lot of flexibility around the other schedules. Figure 5.5 shows a flexibly scheduled week. The fourth- and second-grade lessons are back-to-back with each class's special of the day (see Figure 4.6), whereas the fifth-grade library literacy lessons are taught during their language arts curriculum time and the third grade's library literacy lessons are taught during their social studies curriculum time (see Figure 4.5). The library media specialist also meets with new parent volunteers twice during the week and meets with the principal about the library media budget. The library media specialist will plan with the first-grade team on Thursday and have some planning time of his own on Tuesday, Wednesday, and Thursday. With the shortened week, the first graders will come to the library media center next week.

Figure 5.6 shows another flexible scheduled week.

	Monday	Tuesday	Wednesday	Thursday	Friday
8 - 8:30 8:30 - 9	Prepare Myths		Team Leaders	Plan 1st Grade	
9 - 9:30 9:30 - 10	5A - Myths	KA KB	↓	5B - Myths 5C - Myths	5D - Myths 5A - Draw
10 - 10:30 10:30 - 11	3C - CD-Ref.	3D - CD-Ref.	Admin Time	Planning	3A - CD-Ref. 3B - CD-Ref.
11 - 11:30 11:30 - 12	Pre Hist. Fict.	4C - Hist Fict 4B - Hist Fict	↓	↓ Lunch	Lunch
12 - 12:30 12:30 - 1	Lunch	Lunch Ms. Royo - cam.	Lunch	G.T. Video Taping Ms. Royo	Admin Time
1 - 1:30 1:30 - 2	2D - LA-Ref.	KC KD	Plan 2nd Grade	↓ Clean-up	2A - LA-Ref.
2 - 2:30 2:30 - 3	2A - 4 Regions	4A - Hist Fict 4D - Hist Fict	2B - 4 Regions	2D - 4 Regions	2C - 4 Regions
3 - 3:30 3:30 - 4	Train Ms. Royo Video Cam.		Specials Team Meeting		

Fig. 5.6. Another flexibly scheduled week.

The library media specialist is busy both before and after school. He has learned not to schedule any classes for Wednesday morning right after a team leaders' meeting because he never knows how long they will go. This week the fifth grades will be introduced to their next genre, myths and their library literacy lessons can be back-to-back with their specials because their specials are back-to-back with their language arts time. The next two lessons in this unit call for the fifth graders to learn to use the new drawing program the school purchased and then draw part of a classroom-produced myth. The third graders are coming to the library media center to use CD-ROM references to look up information about the fifty states. Every year, the third graders present the states to the rest of the school. The fourth graders will be starting their language arts unit on historical fiction. Notice the library media specialist gave himself time to prepare for that lesson on Monday. Ms. Royo is coming in to learn how to operate the school's video camera so that she can start taping the gifted and talented projects on Tuesday and Thursday. Some of the second-grade classes are coming in for two different library literacy lessons this week. One lesson was scheduled back-to-back with their special to allow them time to find out more about an author. The teacher will come to the library media center with the students for the other lesson, part of their social studies unit. During this one-hour library literacy lesson, the students will visit four different stations on the four regions of the United States. The teacher will oversee two of the stations, and the library media specialist will oversee the other two. These lessons will be held during their social studies time. The first graders start on their autobiography unit next week and will come to the library media center five times in the next three weeks (see Chapter 4). The band classes, field trips, assemblies, and other special events that are scheduled overlay the library media specialist's schedule.

Half-hour or hour-long library literacy lessons would fit into the school's schedule more easily than fifteen-minute or forty-five-minute lessons because it is based on half-hour increments. Other time frames are doable but would not be a usual occurrence for a lesson time. Individual half-hour library media lessons fit easily before or after a class's special on a day when they have only one special. Even though all the schedules can be overpowering at times, there are ebbs. It is ironic that the library media specialist's schedule is flexible, yet it must dovetail with many other schedules so that its flexibility is tempered.

Fourth, sometimes a library literacy lesson is best taught back-to-back with a class' special so that the teacher or team can have a longer planning time and get some things accomplished such as report cards, conferences, or field-trip preparation. The fourth-grade library literacy lessons on Wednesday and the second-grade lessons on Friday in Figure 5.5 allow the teachers to have a full hour of planning. Giving the teachers this planning time can be a gift from the library media specialist now and then.

A stand-alone library literacy lesson, which is a library literacy lesson of interest but not directly tied to a curriculum unit, is also appropriate when teachers need more planning time. The overall yearly school schedule and the curriculum schedule for units to be taught at each grade level will indicate when stand-alone lessons will be appropriate, as well as timeframes during which planning may be at a minimum and the library media specialist's schedule freer. At these times, it may be best to teach a stand-alone lesson with skills that can transfer to other curriculum lessons later. Examples include appreciation of literature, holiday stories, interesting new general technology programs, new fiction books, or a great lesson that students have always enjoyed but that doesn't currently fit into a particular classroom curriculum. Even if you have a flexible schedule, library literacy lessons might best be taught back-to-back with specials on occasion.

Fifth, integrated library literacy lessons can fit into a schedule as close as possible to the curriculum time if it can't be taught during the curriculum time. In Figure 5.6, the fifth and third grades' library literacy lessons are taught back-to-back with their specials, which are back-to-back with the curriculum unit in which they are working. In these cases, the library media specialist might say, "We'd really like to be teaching this library literacy lesson next period (or last period), when you are in language arts class, but this time fit into our schedule better. Just remember what we are doing right now integrates with your curriculum unit."

Sixth, often library literacy lessons that are integrated with a curriculum unit can be covered in a few weeks' time. The library literacy lessons for the second grade's urban, suburban, and rural unit (see Figure 2.4) amounted to only a one-hour and a half-hour lesson during the social studies curriculum time. The two lessons were easily scheduled in advance to coincide with the end of the social studies unit. The autobiography unit mentioned in Chapters 2 and 4 came in the middle of the six-week-long first-grade unit. It was integrated yet independent of what they were doing in the classroom. The class autobiography needed to be completed by the end of the unit of study, so the library literacy lessons and class work were completed as they fit in. Connecting library literacy lessons to the beginning, middle, or end of a unit readily works into a schedule.

Seventh, if a school wants all library literacy lessons to be integrated and taught in conjunction with a long curriculum unit, this also can be done. Teachers and the library media specialist can work out an equitable system when scheduling classes in this way. Donna B. Miller and J'Lynn Anderson gave examples of fully integrated library media lessons in their book, *Developing an Integrated Library Program* (Miller and Anderson 1994). Having fully integrated library literacy lessons means that the students are using the library media resources as their "textbook" to meet the curriculum's goals. Along the way, they are learning all the information literacy skills involved with accessing, using, and managing the information. A fifth-grade unit that the authors suggested has the class coming to the library media center for three one-hour lessons in the first week; during weeks two and three, they come for three forty-five-minute lessons each week. If there are four or five fifth grades in the school, the plan book fills up fast. The key to fitting all the classes into the library media schedule is to schedule other classes to visit the library media center for the next three or four weeks, while the fifth graders do not come in for that time. During these same weeks, the second grade may be starting a unit in which the students would come to the library media center for four one-hour classes during weeks one and two.

During those weeks until the next unit connected with the library media center, the fifth or second graders would come to the library media center informally, perhaps as a class with their teacher or for a special group in which they are involved. There might be a reading club, special author visit, or other activities that a student can join outside the usual class times or curriculum-related times. Remember that the students will be going to the library media center to check out and return books as well as to work on various classroom assignments, either individually or in small groups. School-wide planning should occur so that the timing of the units involving the library literacy lessons are equitable for all grades over the year. With this schedule, a student may be in the library media center three or more times a week for three weeks straight and then for the next three weeks come in only to check out books or attend special events until a new unit starts. The library media specialist's balancing act starts when she needs to match slow library media center weeks for one grade with busy library media center weeks for another. Many schools want this type of scheduling and make it work well. If flexible access to the library media center is in full swing, the students will still be able to go to the library media center even if it's not for a library literacy lesson. With this type of scheduling, the library media specialist presents students with many information literacy skills during a short time, in connection with a current unit of study.

Eighth, with a flexible schedule, the library media center can accommodate almost any school-wide classroom scheduling scheme. Some schools have full-hour classes, and block scheduling may involve even longer class periods. Schools may wish to have the first forty-five minutes of each day for reading only. If the whole school reads for forty-five minutes everyday, classes can be scheduled to read in the library media center or come in to select books they want to read. Principals may feel that they need to increase planning time for teachers even when it is not in the contract, so the library literacy lesson time may get increased. Furthermore, schools may wish to stress technology and the production of media. In all cases, the first priority is still to create lifelong learners, readers, and library users, and the library literacy lessons and the classroom lessons are the two main ways to accomplish that goal. Both the library media schedule and the classroom schedule need to be kept flexible around the many scheduling requests. The library media specialist should be considered a resource teacher, and not scheduled as a "special" to cover teachers' planning times; but certainly additional teachers' planning time is made available as classes are scheduled in the library media center. Look again at the suggestions in Figure 4.15 where through the expanded flexible library media schedule teachers actually have more scheduled library literacy lessons for their students. All in all, it is best to think of the classroom schedules and the library media schedule together and plan secondary priorities around both of these schedules.

The ideal library media schedule can be seen in a plan book. The ideal is when students are engaged in a library media lesson with the library media center's resources and personnel when they need to learn or experience the needed information or skill. As much as possible, the students must be able to come into the library media center at time of need and learn skills when they are needed. Flexibility is a must if lifelong learners, readers, and library users are to be created.

A Useful Plan Book Can Be Created

A school library media specialist's plan book is unique. It needs to include more than just what will be taught that week, as a teacher's plan book would include. A library media specialist's plan book needs to have information about all the grades, units of study, and the general school information, too. When I began planning with the teachers at Waterloo Elementary School, I wanted to do it just right, so I started carrying around notebooks, curriculum guides, and a plan book. So many books were overwhelming to the teacher, I never really found just what I needed in the guides, and I always forgot something so I ended up with just one good-sized plan book. I filled in everything that I did in a day and knew that each day would be different than the one before or the one following. A library media specialist working with flexible scheduling can create a plan book filled with everything she'll need. Here are some suggestions of what should go into a library media specialist's plan book.

First, an all-in-one plan book can be created with some cutting and pasting.

Second, it is best to write everything into the plan book.

Third, lunch and planning times are never the same time each day or each week; that's the way the flexible schedule works.

Fourth, the school library media specialist's schedule changes daily.

Fifth, because teachers are used to having a set schedule, the school library media specialist needs to help them get used to having library literacy lessons on a flexible schedule.

Sixth, the library media specialist is in charge of the library media schedule, although it may not seem so.

Fig. 5.7. Ways to create a library media specialist's plan book.

    First, an all-in-one plan book can be created with some cutting and pasting. Everything the library media specialist needs to have on hand for planning with the teachers can be incorporated into just one plan book. The plan book needs to have pockets dividers, one for each grade, where one can place ideas, curriculum lists, past lesson sheets, teachers' skills sheets, novel lists, book report forms, and anything the teacher has shared with the library media specialist. Some of these lists may need to be reduced in size to fit in the pocket.

    Figure 5.8 shows the pocket divider for the third grade. Listed on the pocket are the science and social studies curriculums, plus a listing of the books from which the teachers may select class-wide reading books. In the pocket is a list of the library literacy lessons taught to the third graders last year, a curriculum skills overview sheet prepared by the county, and assorted other slips of paper. Having all these papers immediately available comes in handy. Having the specials schedule, as well as other schedules such as school holiday, field trip, and conference schedules, in the plan book or written in on the days they will occur is also helpful. All this information fits in the plan book if it is listed succinctly. A full, well-organized, and compact plan book is most helpful to any library media specialist.

    Second, it is best to write everything into the plan book. Include events such as holidays, field trips, assemblies, testing, and other scheduled events to alert the library media specialist that those days will be different. Exact times of events and lessons can be important, for sometimes a lesson is squeezed in around a field trip or an assembly. If the library media specialist has any school duties, those need to be filled in. When library literacy lessons are being planned it's difficult to remember that something specific happens every Tuesday at lunch. It is better to write lunch duty in on every Tuesday in the plan book. Figures 5.2, 5.3, 5.5, and 5.6 show examples of flexible schedules. On those schedules, the library media specialist has written in many events in addition to classes. Unless a school is overcrowded, there is enough time in the week for each class to generally have one library literacy lesson and for the library media specialist to have planning and administrative time.

CURRICULUM OVERVIEW
Affective Domain Language Literature

Classes Taught in the Library
1st Quarter 3rd grade, 2000

Orientation - 3 lessons   Realistic Fic char
Maps NSEW scale   Maps Lat and Log
Dict. guide wds   Use atlases - 4 diff
Outcomes for Reading project - possibilities

2nd Quarter

Ancestors   3 Reasons- How to

Story Elements

Setting - where & when the story takes place

Plot - the main events of the story

Conflict - the main problem in the story

Resolution - how the problem or conflict was solved

Climax - the higest point of excitement

Theme - the author's message

*

SCIENCE
1: Life Cycle of Plants
2: Experimentation
3: Energy - Simple Circuits
4: Weather

SOCIAL STUDIES
Life in Howard Co.
Learning about No.Am.
Investigating the World

TRADE BOOKS FOR GRADE 3
How a Book Is Made by Aliki
Julian's Glorius Summer by Ann Cameron
Molly's Pilgrim by Barbara Cohen
Mufaro's Beautiful Daughter by John Steptoe
Muggie Maggie by Beverly Cleary
Paul Bunyan by Steven Kellogg
Shoeshine Girl by Clyde Robert Bulla

Fig. 5.8. The all-in-one plan book.

Third, lunch and planning times are never the same time each day or each week; that's the way the flexible schedule works. Because the library media specialist does not want to forget them, it may be best to write in lunch and planning times as lesson times are about half filled. If the library media specialist says "no" to the library literacy lesson times the teacher suggests, the teacher will get frustrated especially if the "no" is said because the library media specialist will be at lunch. In that case, the library media specialist should move lunchtime and teach the class. In many cases, a class can only come for a library literacy lesson one or two times during a week because of all the other things scheduled for them. In that case, the library media specialist wants to be able to see them when they can come in, so the library media specialist's lunch and planning time may have to be placed in another time slot. The library media specialist also can place lessons together to make the schedule more efficient by asking a teacher if the class might be able to come in at another time so that there will be a half day to get a book order completed, for example. Professional conference days also need to be written in. After scheduling for a quarter, a library media specialist will see how scheduling library literacy lessons, eating lunch, planning, and having administrative time all fit together. Over a month's time, everything evens out. The plan book should include everything with which the library media specialist is involved and that the school is doing.

Fourth, the school library media specialist's schedule changes daily. With a fixed schedule, every week is the same, but with a flexible schedule, every day is different. The lack of routine is another reason the plan book is vital. It is best for the library media specialist to check her plan book before she goes home to get an idea of what the next day will be like. There just might be a meeting first thing the next day and a class right after that!

Fifth, because teachers are used to having a set schedule, the school library media specialist needs to help them get used to having library literacy lessons on a flexible schedule. Giving verbal reminders each morning by walking to classrooms or seeing teachers in the office helps them remember that they have "library media" that day. Reminding the teachers also will help the library media specialist get ready for the day. With such a flexible library media center schedule, it might be helpful to post it in the library media center and in the office because operating on a different schedule everyday is not a usual pattern for most people. Having a schedule that does not stay the same is a challenge for the library media specialist, the teachers, and the school.

Sixth, the library media specialist is in charge of the library media schedule although it may not seem so. The library media schedule does come in second to the school schedules, but the library media specialist is still in control of the library media schedule and its management; it is not in charge of the library media specialist. By the second semester, the library media specialist will see that in fact she does have control over schedules and classes. There are plenty of opportunities to teach lessons and to extend them. They do not all have to be taught immediately. The overall thrust of the library media program is to teach certain skills in a year. Luckily, if they are not completed in the first year, they can be added the next year. The library media schedule may seem to take on a life of its own, but the library media specialist can keep it in check, manipulate it, and make sure there's enough time for everything.

Administrative Time Can Be Pinpointed

Administrative time is in the library media specialist's schedule, but it needs to be pinpointed each week. This is the time the library media specialist needs to actually run the library media center. This is not planning time, which also needs to be scheduled. Finding administrative time is where the library media specialist can be creative and well organized. Being well organized may be of primary importance because when the library media specialist finds administrative time, she will want to use it wisely.

The Weekly Schedule Can Help

Administrative time can be found in the weekly schedule. If there are four fifth-grade classes and four third-grade classes, and if on Tuesdays most classes in those grades have specials, then administrative time can be planned for the first two periods on Tuesdays. In Figures 5.2, 5.3, and 5.5, administrative time is scheduled for Tuesdays. Because of other schedules, administrative time is not on the Figure 5.6 schedule on Tuesday but is on Wednesday. When the school schedule is created, it is best to configure at least one day when all the classes in a grade are out at specials so the team can have joint planning time. Perhaps the same is true one afternoon a week as well. Figure 4.6 shows that on Tuesday afternoon, all but two classes are out at specials for an hour. On Tuesday afternoon, only 2C or 1B would sign up for a lesson or a third-, fourth-, or fifth-grade class because every other class is at a special. It is hoped for that those classes could find other times to have their library literacy lesson. If so, the library media specialist could easily have two full hours for administrative time on Tuesday from 1 to 3 p.m. If the library media specialist can find two hours together twice a week, that may be better than four one-hour slots spread throughout a week. Looking at the schedule in Figure 4.6, the library media specialist could probably plan a whole administrative day every couple of months on a Tuesday.

Figure 5.9, on page 76, shows a week's schedule in which the library media specialist took advantage of the two times on Tuesday when almost half of the school is busy at specials as well as time on Friday afternoon. If all the administrative items and duties are well organized, the library media specialist can use her time effectively for those two-hour periods. Parent volunteers can do many tasks in the library media center (see Chapter 3), so it's worth the library media specialist's times to organize those tasks during her administrative time. The weekly schedule provides natural places where administrative time can be found.

Special Days Provide Administrative Time

Special events always seem to be held in the library media center. Grandparent's Day, school picture day, and field day can provide the library media specialist with a whole day of administrative time. If class pictures are taken in the library media center, it is easy to say that library literacy lessons cannot be scheduled that day (see Figure 5.9). If a library literacy lesson was a must, then the library media specialist can go to the classroom, but usually the classroom schedule is also upset because of the picture taking. Knowing when there will be a "special" day helps the library media specialist schedule a much-needed full day of administrative time.

	Monday	Tuesday	Wednesday	Thursday	Friday
8 - 8:30 8:30 - 9				School Picture Day in the Library	
9 - 9:30 9:30 - 10		Administrative Time			
10 - 10:30 10:30 - 11		↓			
11 - 11:30 11:30 - 12					
12 - 12:30 12:30 - 1					
1 - 1:30 1:30 - 2		Administrative Time			Administrative Time
2 - 2:30 2:30 - 3		↓		↓	↓
3 - 3:30 3:30 - 4					

Fig. 5.9. Pinpointed administrative time.

Administrative Time Can Be
Written in When Needed

If an administrative afternoon is needed, there is nothing wrong with the library media specialist blocking out an hour or two on a given day. When time is needed to take care of a book order, organize parent volunteers, organize for weeding the collection, train new library media helpers, or prepare the budget, administrative time can be blocked out in the plan book. It is best to schedule that kind of administrative time around the project or responsibility. When the library media specialist does this, the school community is more understanding about being unable to schedule library literacy lessons that day. When a full administrative day is planned, rest assured that something will come up that will take time from the planned project. Again, the library media specialist needs to remain flexible and find administrative time in the schedules.

Becoming like the Day School means fully instituting flexible access and fully utilizing flexible scheduling. It seems like everything connected with the library media center gets expanded and extended when full flexible access is provided. Likewise, the library media schedule is different every day and every week when flexible scheduling is fully used. The library media specialist relies on her plan book to know what to do next and manages the schedule to fit the needs of the classroom schedules, the library literacy lessons, lunch, planning, and administrative time. Becoming like the Day School creates lifelong learners, readers, and library users because access to the library media center and library literacy lesson schedule work around the needs of the students.

Chapter 6

PLANNING AHEAD FOR SUCCESS

The Afternoon School's administrative team, its library media specialist, and its key teachers have continued their conversation about becoming a school like the Day School. They realize that a lot of changes need to take place to work toward the goal of creating lifelong learners, readers, and library users, and they are ready to move ahead. This is what they are saying.

Yes, I'm convinced!
Let's do it!
Let's make the move. Let's create lifelong learners, readers, and library users!
Let's raise the academic achievement of our students.
Let's be like the Day School.
Yes, let's make changes in our school!

Changes!!! Changes??? Do we have to make channnnges???

Change is the only thing of which everyone can be sure, but the only one who likes a change is a baby with a wet diaper. Change is constant, but change is also manageable.

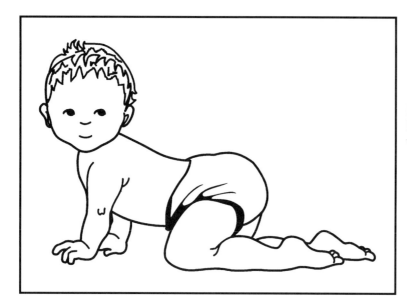

Fig. 6.1. The only one who likes a change is a baby with a wet diaper.

If you, as a school administrator, library media specialist, educator, or member of the school community want to create lifelong learners, readers, and library users and raise your students' academic achievement, you will need to make changes in your school. It is easier to deal with change in the school or in the library media center if you understand what change is and some of its finer points. Being aware of how others have dealt with a changeover to flexible access and scheduling and in what ways one needs to remain flexible will aid library media specialists in making decisions.

UNDERSTANDING CHANGE

There always seem to be changes occurring in the educational world, so it's easy to find information about making changes in the school setting. Change occurs when someone becomes dissatisfied enough with the status quo to want some alternative options. That person then has a vision of how the change will make it better for them and starts to outline the steps that need to be taken to get there. It may be lower-than-expected test scores; a district directive; an idea from a journal article, book, or conference session; or a grant proposal opportunity that gives the spark necessary to light the "change" fire.

First, the principal plays a most important role in the change process.

Second, one person needs to be dissatisfied enough to challenge the status quo.

Third, an intriguing vision needs to be developed and shared with the staff.

Fourth, clear and practical steps for the change are outlined.

Fifth, any disadvantages to the changes should be presented.

Sixth, opportunities for feedback are built into the change process.

Seventh, the benefits of change, which are shared, need to outweigh the costs of change.

Eighth, staff development for all those involved in the change process is very important.

Ninth, making physical changes to the library media center or resource collection highlight the fact that changes are happening.

Fig. 6.2. Nine steps to change.

According to Ken Haycock, "The principal is the single most important player in the change process and plays a direct and active role in leading any process of change by becoming familiar with the nature of the change and by working with staff to develop, execute, and monitor a school implementation plan" (Haycock 1999, p. 19). Furthermore, the authors of *Lessons from Library Power* stated, "One important element [to help a school focus on intellectual quality] appears to be the . . . strength of leadership [of the principal] in pushing and helping faculty grapple with issues surrounding the improvement of teaching and learning. A central role for a principal is prompting and facilitating staff dialogue over key issues. . . . While a principal alone may not move a faculty toward a strong professional community, that person's efforts probably make a great difference" (Zweizig and McAfee Hopkins 1999, p. 163). Whoever provides the initial leadership to make changes in a school, it is wise to enlist the principal's support as one of the first steps. The principal plays an important role in a school's change process.

There are many steps involved when making changes in a school. In her article, "The Challenge to Change," Doris Vanek (Vanek 1994), coordinator of the staff development program for the Howard County Public School System, outlined six steps to take when implementing change. She suggested, based on her readings, that if a school wants to make changes, the school community must challenge the status quo. The person leading the way for change, the change agent, needs to help others feel as dissatisfied with the way things are being done or are going as they are. In her article, "Implementing Change: What School Library Media Specialists Should Know," Sandra Hughes-Hassell (Hughes-Hassell 2001) listed the characteristics for the change agent. She stated that change agents need to be knowledgeable about the changes to be made, the people involved, the school's organization, and other factors, and how the change process works. Hughes-Hassell went on to explain that various other authors on the subject have suggested that the change agent must possess effective leadership skills and abilities, have a positive attitude, and be able to work effectively with people.

Next, a new vision needs to be developed by the change agent and that vision needs to intrigue the staff and raise their interest. Furthermore, clear and practical steps to make the changes need to be identified. The staff needs to be reassured that this plan is well thought out and that the change will be a lasting one. People dislike a stressful and uncertain transition through change. Additionally, Ms. Vanek suggested that the disadvantages of the change should be presented. She stated that it is better to have negative possibilities on the table than to have them come up later. Certainly, opportunities for feedback need to be built into the whole process. These steps, as they are being implemented, may need to be adjusted along the way as feedback is given. Furthermore, the benefits of the changes should be clearly outlined. Staff members will change if the benefits outweigh the costs of change. However many steps there may be to implement changes in your school, they need to be carefully developed.

The Library Power experience suggests that staff development is another step to take to make successful changes in a school setting. Staff development for all involved in Library Power schools proved to be very beneficial. The program came into schools to create change and reform from the library media center out into the school. They used flexible access and scheduling as the means to push the rest of the school to develop resource-based curriculums, promote collaboration among staff, and increase awareness and utilization of the library media center and the library media specialist while improving the teaching and learning process. The Library Power schools could not have had the successes that they had or will continue to have without staff development. The Library Power library media specialists participated in at least twenty different in-service sessions over the years their schools were involved in the program. The professional development that Library Power provided was successful not only with the library media specialists, but also many teachers and principals. Because staff development promotes continual learning, Library Power found that it was a key ingredient for successful change. One Library Power director said, "Staff Development caused more change that anything else we did" (Zweizig and McAfee Hopkins 1999, p. 163).

Furthermore, the Library Power program provided funding so that physical changes could take place in the schools through renovations to the library media center as well as the purchase of new materials. "Library Power provides concrete forms of assistance in new books, a professional librarian, and the innovation of collaboration on collection and instruction. Rallying around such concrete assistance can provide a school with the basis for building agreement about purpose and working collectively to improve instruction" (Zweizig and McAfee Hopkins 1999, p. 129). These concrete forms of assistance are easily visible first steps indicating that things would be different. Even when there is not a influx of funds to a school to promote physical changes, schools have found other ways to visualize the changes by weeding the library media and classroom collections, rearranging rooms, moving staff to different grade levels, incorporating total school themes and activities, or bringing new administrators on board. Highlighting the fact that changes are taking place is always a good step to take.

Cindy Jeffery Krimmelbein's book, *The Choice to Change: Establishing an Integrated School Library Media Program* (Krimmelbein 1989), provides readers with a great deal of information about change. She explained how to go about it personally, if need be, as well as within a school so that an integrated skills program is the outcome. The book is an excellent resource.

The authors of the book *Lessons from Library Power* (Zweizig and McAfee Hopkins 1999) have provided readers with further insight into the change process. They noted that there are two kinds of change—an organizational restructuring change, in which specific steps can be taken to implement concepts such as flexible access and flexible scheduling, and a cultural change, in which beliefs and behaviors are changed (for example, making changes to create lifelong learners, readers, and library users). Organizational change is, of course, easier to implement than cultural change, and organizational change is usually the means to the cultural changes. Flexible access and flexible scheduling are two successful and validated organizational changes that help, facilitate and support the cultural change of creating lifelong learners, readers, and library users, as well as other cultural changes such as curriculum development, the integration of skills, and collaboration among a school's staff.

Another interesting delineation about change comes in a chapter (by Jean Brown) from Ken Haycock's book, "Navigating the '90s—The Teacher-Librarian as Change Agent" (Brown 1999). In the article, she pointed out that there are "high consensus" schools where teachers openly cooperate with each other and never stop learning how to teach and there are "low consensus" schools where teachers work in isolation and do not feel a part of the professional community. At a conference years ago, I picked up a "Reaction to Change" survey (author unknown) that, after it was taken, would indicate how a person would accept change. This survey suggested five categories regarding the ability to accept change. An innovator is eager to try new ideas, take risks, but may be considered a little crazy by the rest of the staff. "Leaders," also open to change, are more thoughtful and therefore trusted by staff. The staff members who are the "early majority" are deliberate about their decisions to follow the leaders and to make the changes. The "late minority" of followers are set in their ways and need peer pressure or administrative expectations to make them change and "late adopters" are usually isolated from the rest of the professional community. All school staffs will have staff members in each of these categories.

The early majority and late minority people may fit in those particular categories because they see the transition to the new vision as stressful and uncertain. Their acceptance of the change and willingness to work with it can be encouraged if they feel their needs are heard and addressed, if they don't feel labeled as "holdouts" for the old ways, and if their concerns are incorporated into the change process. Additionally, the authors of *Lessons from Library Power* stated that "the more complex an innovation, the more likely that teachers will resist its adoption. Some research found that teachers go through stages of concern about an innovation; initial resistance is followed by increasing acceptance and adoption as teachers become more familiar and comfortable with new practices" (Zweizig and McAfee Hopkins 1999, p. 161). The authors also noted that for change to occur, external support and reinforcement must be present to encourage any change. This support must continue until teachers become comfortable with the new expectations and practices. In the case of Library Power, the whole program reinforced the changes being made. School district, parents' committees, governmental agencies, and businesses provided the needed support to the school. With internal and external support, schools can make changes that are lasting and beneficial.

Educational changes take forethought. They can't just happen overnight or without any planning. Those who are instituting changes in a school are wise to orchestrate the changes in their school.

LEARNING FROM OTHERS

The process of making changes in a school is easier if those involved learn from the experience of others. Some of the factors that are involved in making the changeover to flexible access and flexible scheduling are within the library media specialist's control, and other factors involve the participation and support of others in the school community. Let's take a look at what lessons can be learned from the experience of others.

There Are Change Factors That Are Within the Library Media Specialist's Control

There are change factors over which the library media specialist has control. The following are some examples that other library media specialists thought were important to the success of their changeover to flexible access and flexible scheduling.

First, flexible access and flexible scheduling need to be kept in perspective.

Second, staff development for the library media specialist and other school community members is necessary and most helpful.

Third, some of the variables such as school size and staff size at a school need to be considered.

Fourth, it is easiest to implement flexible access, flexible scheduling, or both with the primary grades.

Fifth, a listing of essential information literacy skills clarifies what the library media specialist will be teaching.

Sixth, change takes time and patience.

Fig. 6.3. Change factors that are within the library media specialist's control.

First, flexible access and flexible scheduling need to be kept in perspective. This is among the first lessons a library media specialist can learn from others in the field. Flexible access and flexible scheduling are means to an end, not an end in themselves. Many library media specialists in the 1980s wanted "to have flexible scheduling." We thought that if we had flexible scheduling, we would also have the integration of library media center skills and planning with teachers. If we had started with integrating library media center skills as our only goal, planning with teachers and flexible scheduling would have logically followed. When we asked for flexible scheduling, it appeared as if we were asking for special favors from the administrators when all we really wanted was not to teach library literacy skills in isolation. It is best to look at the whole school program and work toward its goals rather than focus only on flexible access and flexible scheduling.

Second, staff development for the library media specialist and other school community members is necessary and most helpful. Staff development appears to be the best avenue to give library media specialists and others the opportunity to redefine their roles and routines so they can assume a leadership role in a school. Strong leadership from the library media specialist is a necessity when making the changeover to flexible access and scheduling, as is explained in Chapter 3. A strong leader is one who knows where he or she is going and how to get there. This does not mean a leader must stand up and give a speech at every staff meeting. It simply says that a leader needs a clear direction and then works toward it. Others will follow. Being a strong leader requires a focused sense of direction.

To duplicate the staff development situation that was available to the Library Power schools takes some planning and coordination. Their staff development opportunities were available in abundance, and through them library media specialists became part of a team effort. They no longer felt isolated in their schools. Perhaps staff development opportunities can be created for library media specialists who desire them either at the district level or at a state level. It also appears that just one or two sessions are not enough, but a series of sessions over time needs to be developed. Having staff development provides the feeling of broad support for change that is necessary to begin change and to maintain the changes made. If staff development is not available, then administrative support and the library media specialist's strong leadership become even more important when flexible access and flexible scheduling are instituted in a single school (see Browne 1989 and Ohlrich 1991).

Third, some of the variables such as school and staff size at a school need to be considered. These are not under the library media specialist's control, but how he works with them is. Many library media specialists are still responsible for two schools or more; some have overcrowded schools; and some, being new to the field or to a school, are just learning about their collection and their students' names. Split classes are also a variable that complicates many things in a school. If in assessing a school's situation the library media specialist finds that fully implementing flexible access and flexible scheduling is not realistic, then he can try implementing parts of one or both ideas. Taking on a realistic challenge will increase the likelihood that it can be met.

Fourth, it may be easiest to implement flexible access, flexible scheduling, or both with the primary grades. As those classes move up through the grades, the flexibility that the students have come to expect goes with them to the next grade level. Primary students are easily taught that the library media center is the place to go for information because they are not used to another situation. Yes, primary teachers generally have a lot of books in their classrooms for free-reading time, but through the years, I've found they can also be convinced to send their students over to the library media center as a center time to have access to even more books. With the primary grades, it is easy to integrate information literacy skills into lessons such as an author a month, cooking with books, or other thematic unit. I found that the primary students were the ones who loved to check out books every day and couldn't wait to check out the nonfiction books "over there." The schedule in the primary grades is probably more flexible than that in the intermediate classes, so different lesson times fit in fine. Certainly intermediate students should be using the library media center more often, and some flexibility with those grades can be achieved. It is best to start with success, and allowing primary students to go in and out of the library media center independently is a success for them and the school.

Fifth, a listing of essential information literacy skills clarifies what the library media specialist will be teaching. Chapter 7 includes a listing of essential skills. The first time I suggested that the information literacy skills ("library media skills") be integrated into the classroom curriculum at Whiskey Bottom Road Elementary School in Laurel, Maryland, a teacher asked, "What do you teach?" My quick answer was, "You know, things you need to know about the library media center," but that was not an adequate answer for the teacher. A classroom teacher also teaches many "library media skills." At first, that may be confusing to both the teacher and the library media specialist, but the overlap provides reasons to integrate and collaborate in the teaching of those skills.

Sixth, change takes time and patience. Changing over to flexible access, flexible scheduling, or both is not something that is done in one month and then works well after that. Those initiating the change process will find that they need to work at maintaining the initial "September" enthusiasm for the concepts in themselves and in others. A way to do this might be to start with a limited program. Because many library media specialists found that the most challenging aspect of the changeover was the cooperative planning and evaluating lessons with teachers, it might be wise to start with one grade level and allow the program to grow as staff members adjust to flexible scheduling and planning for it. Others have found that integrating information skills for all students at every grade level was difficult. Again, starting small and expanding the program might be wise. Some library media specialists found that it was difficult to provide adequate library media center staff, resources, and the kind of services that teachers and students desired. Creating a positive demand for library media services can lead to additional support, which pushes for additional staffing. Building a flexible library media program takes time, dedication, and some adjustments.

The library media specialist can control many factors related to making the changeover to flexible access and flexible scheduling. Library media specialists can be prepared if they learn from the experiences of others.

There Are Change Factors That Need the Support of Others

A library media specialist needs the support of others in the school and on the "change team" to implement some changes. Marilyn K. Oswald's research for her master's degree at Minnesota State University in Mankato suggested that, "Administrative commitment, teacher cooperation, effective communications, and strong leadership by the library media specialist encompass the most important elements in determining the degree of success elementary school library media programs will achieve with flexible scheduling" (Oswald 1994, p. 27). All these factors are important, but only the library media specialists' "strong leadership" is under their control. The other factors involve the support or cooperation of others—administrative team, staff, and the school community. The following are areas in which support is needed or where the library media specialist must gain support:

First, administrative support and commitment to flexible access, flexible scheduling, or both is a must.

Second, gaining teacher cooperation is a concern for library media specialists implementing flexible access and flexible scheduling.

Third, teachers' support of the concepts increases when equity is not an issue.

Fourth, maintaining a good trust level between the library media specialist and the school community is vital.

Fifth, some teachers are not sold on the flexible access and flexible scheduling concepts until they have gained some experience with them.

Sixth, effective communications to everyone in the school community is a must.

Seventh, the broader school community must be called on for support.

Fig. 6.4. Change factors that need the support of others.

First, administrative support and commitment to flexible access, flexible scheduling, or both, is a must (see "Understanding Change" in this chapter). In the end, flexible access and flexible scheduling create changes in how the students and school community learn and work together. It is important that the administration of the school understand how the concepts of flexible access and flexible scheduling create lifelong learners, readers, and library users so that they, like the library media specialist, keep the concepts in perspective and focus. Administrative support is necessary for far-reaching changes to occur.

Second, gaining teacher cooperation is a concern for library media specialists implementing flexible access and flexible scheduling. Seventy-four percent of the respondents to a survey conducted by Ms. Oswald (Oswald 1994, p. 27) said it was their top concern. To gain the teachers' cooperation, some library media specialists went out of their way to assure that their cooperation would be secured. Compromising and adjusting are two necessary things to do when working with others. A library media specialist also can start with some teachers and let the good ideas grow. Others will want to join in; they just need time or a gentle suggestion to try something new. It is important that a certain level of trust is built and continues to build between the library media specialist and the teaching staff. With trust, teachers will work with the new concepts.

Third, teachers' support of the concepts increases when equity in not an issue. With classes and activities no longer on a fixed schedule, some teachers worry that their class will not receive the usual number of library literacy lessons. There are many variables involved in flexible scheduling, but the number of times classes at each grade level come to the library media center for a lesson should not be one of them. Throughout my career as a library media specialist, if I taught a lesson with one third-grade class, I taught it or a similar one to all third grades. Over a month's time, every class in a grade was in the library media center for the same amount of time doing the same type of lessons. If one class made a video, the others did as well. I know I went out of my way to make sure that the reluctant teacher's class had the lessons, too. I might even have kept that teacher on a fixed schedule most of the time so the students would not miss an opportunity to visit the library media center. I wanted every student to have the same experience with the library media program. Building equity into the program continues to build trust between the library media specialist and the teaching staff.

Fourth, maintaining a good trust level between the library media specialist and the school community is vital. Changing to flexible access and flexible scheduling are organizational changes, and therefore easier than cultural changes, but there are underlying cultural changes involved. Teachers may ask what will happen if the library media specialist is not scheduled each day and whether he will still be teaching as often. If the library media specialist is not scheduled each day, will every class still have "library media," or will some classes have it more often? The library media specialist can alleviate fears that he is sitting in his office doing nothing by posting his schedule for the week.

With the integration of skills, the library media specialist becomes aware of what is or is not happening in the classroom. With collaboration, the library media specialist now becomes aware of what is or is not written in the plan book. With flexible scheduling, the library media specialist becomes aware of classroom schedules and activities. With this new knowledge, the library media specialist should keep any information about a teacher to himself, speak only of the positive, and be the first to praise the classroom teacher to the administration. With collaboration, the library media specialist will also become a co-teacher with the classroom teacher. The library media specialist's expected role changes, and the acceptance of the new role may take some time. Trust is an ideal that is built upon each day.

Fifth, Douglas L. Zweizig and Dianne McAfee Hopkins noted in *Lessons from Library Power* (1999) that some teachers were not sold on the flexible access and flexible scheduling concepts until they had gained experience with them. The teachers needed to see that making the change to these concepts benefited them and their class. Many teachers stay with the status quo because it is comfortable and secure. If it is desired that all teachers make changes then those staff members need to know the change will have a positive impact, that it will be supported by the administration and parents, and that there will be training and collaboration throughout the transition. If the total school is focused on a goal to improve the school overall, making some organizational changes such as flexible access and flexible scheduling can fall into place as a means to achieve the larger school goal.

Sixth, effective communications to everyone in the school community is a must. Linthicum Elementary School in Linthicum, Maryland, prepared a three-page handout (Wilson 1993) for their school community—staff, students, parents, and district level administrators—under the direction of Bonnie Wilson, the library media specialist. It detailed definitions, goals, objectives, policies, and procedures. The handout gave examples of lessons, described cooperative planning, and provided additional information. Mrs. Wilson and her principal realized that some teachers might file a grievance regarding the changeover to flexible scheduling, so they were prepared. They collected data to present to the faculty and parents at the end of the year showing that classes actually came to the library media center for more hours under flexible scheduling than they did under fixed scheduling, which settled that issue. Other schools have produced similar information sheets and presentations. It is particularly important that any communication about the library media program be available at all times and updated often.

Seventh, the broader school community must be called on for support. If other schools in the district or state are having success in implementing changes, including switching to flexible access or flexible scheduling, it is helpful for all involved to connect with that school. The Library Power (Zweizig and McAfee Hopkins 1999) experience points to the fact that having the support of the school district, government officials, businesses, and the general population is necessary if any program is to permeate the educational system and continue to broaden the students' educational experiences. It is important to have the support of others in the school community for flexible access and flexible scheduling to be successful.

A school library media specialist can learn a great deal from those who have already made the changeover to flexible access and flexible scheduling. There are things he can control and things he can influence. In the end, a changeover to flexible access and flexible scheduling should be a team effort, benefiting from the cooperation of the school's administration, the library media specialist, key teachers, other members of the immediate school community, and from the broader school community.

REMAINING FLEXIBLE

There are many factors involved with implementing flexible access and flexible scheduling. It is hoped that those in charge of guiding the change process will consider from many angles any problematic situations that arise and then find a solution. If the library media center needs another staff person, then they can look for ways to hire one. If the library media specialist is concerned about his administrative time, he can use the flexibility of the schedule to his advantage. If the changes are taking more time than expected, a three- or five-year plan can be outlined; if the integration of skills and collaboration are moving slowly, the library media specialist can plan lessons alone. There are many instances that encourage a school community to be flexible and open minded about flexible access and flexible scheduling. Remaining flexible about additional developments ensures the success of the changeover to flexible access and flexible scheduling.

First, many of the tasks surrounding the management of the library media center may need to be completed by others to free the library media specialist's time for collaboration and teaching.

Second, the library media specialist may voice concern over the perceived loss of her scheduled administrative time.

Third, the impact of a new school-wide goal may take three or five years to be noted.

Fourth, members of the school community need to understand that every lesson may not be integrated with the curriculum or that the collaboration to prepare a lesson may not be done around a conference table.

Fifth, everyone in a school must adjust to the new flexibility in the school library media center.

Fig. 6.5. Things to remain flexible about.

First, as stated in Chapter 3, many of the tasks surrounding the management of the library media center may need to be completed by others to free the library media specialist's time for collaboration and teaching. Parent volunteers are wonderful, but it would be even better to have the same person every day. When school-based management was implemented at Waterloo Elementary School in Columbia, Maryland, we were allowed the budgetary flexibility to hire an assistant. The number of students at Waterloo Elementary School did not warrant the hiring of an assistant by county guidelines, but we needed one. We used some school funds but mostly book fair profits to pay the assistant's wages. That possibility of hiring an assistant opened up only under school-based management. Having an assistant improved the library media center's service.

Second, the library media specialist may voice concern over the perceived loss of his scheduled administrative time. In reality, as outlined in Chapter 5, there can be more administrative time, and more class time when the schedule is under the library media specialist's control. As library media specialist Becky Roesch of McClave, Colorado, said in response to a questionnaire, "The most important part of flexible scheduling is the 'flexible' library media specialist." Managing a library media center when the library media specialist is adding many other responsibilities to the school day must be met with flexibility.

Third, the impact of a new school-wide goal may take three or five years to be noted. Any change needs to build on itself, and participants may need to make adjustments along the way. It takes time to integrate information literacy skills into the classroom curriculum and to work collaboratively with teachers. Each year lessons get better through the adjustments that the staff makes, and each year the staff finds it easier to work together. It is best to work within the three- or five-year plan and celebrate each area of growth and accomplishment along the way.

Those who want it to all happen "right now" need to learn patience and allow the changes to take hold gradually. Saying in the beginning that the changes will take three or five years to implement helps the process of change by providing realistic expectations.

Fourth, members of the school community need to understand that every lesson may not be integrated with the curriculum or that the collaboration to prepare a lesson may not be done around a conference table. At the start of the changeover, the library media specialist can come to the teachers with lessons that need input from the teachers. If the library media specialist is flexible about integrating lessons into the classroom curriculum and planning with teachers, it puts everyone's mind at ease. If the library media specialist is overly concerned about process, it will cloud the results that benefit the students. Integration of library lessons and the planning of collaborative lessons are good teaching practices. New teachers generally appreciate collaborating on lessons because it decreases the workload and helps them learn about the curriculum. Being flexible about the processes of integration and collaboration will help to ensure their success.

Fifth, everyone in a school must adjust to the new flexibility in the school library media center. For example, flexible access forces a change in the fire-drill procedure because students could be in the library media center at any time during the day and cannot be allowed to go back to class when the fire alarm rings. Flexible scheduling means that a class might be in the library media center rather than in the classroom, although it is not written on the master schedule. Both flexible access and flexible scheduling provide the opportunity for a school to "go with the flow," which may be uncomfortable for some members of the school community. The students' needs cannot always be scheduled, although many educators would like them to be.

It will take three to five years to realize all the benefits of flexible access and flexible scheduling. Groundwork, careful development of a vision, and the commitment of the administration to the concepts are necessary before a change agent should even suggest a change. All aspects of any changeover need to be communicated to the staff with an openness that promotes feedback. Adjustments need to be made throughout the change process. As the goals are implemented in stages, the importance of evaluation and celebration should not be overlooked; within the school setting, there is always the opportunity for a fresh start next September or next semester. The results of all this hard work and planning will be realized. Change is not easy, but it is rewarding. It takes time and careful monitoring for it to go well. For any school to be like the Day School will take many changes, but the changes are manageable.

Chapter 7

INTEGRATING INFORMATION LITERACY SKILLS INTO THE CLASSROOM CURRICULUM

T he Afternoon School's change team is continuing its conversation in the conference room. Things are going well at the school. They are making progress to become more like the Day School.

> Okay! We're making changes at our school.
> We're taking steps to become like the Day School.
> We've agreed on our school-wide goals, the library media specialist is making some changes in the library media center, and we're implementing some flexible access and flexible scheduling to see what possibilities they can offer the school.
> The library media center's been renovated, new materials have been purchased, staff development is underway, the principal's guiding the staff to make many school-wide changes, and we're ready to start integrating information literacy skills into the classroom curriculum.
> We also want to make sure that the students will be able to apply what they've learned in the library literacy lessons to other areas. We want to teach for transfer!
> Yes, that's what we want! We want to start integrating information literacy skills into the classroom curriculum and teaching for transfer.

With the integration of information literacy skills into the classroom curriculum, library literacy and classroom lessons have more meaning. Through the process of integrating information literacy skills, a school's curriculum is streamlined, and the integrated lessons stand a better chance of teaching precisely what the students need to know now. In other words, the integration of information literacy skills into the classroom curriculum facilitates teaching for transfer. When lessons are taught for transfer to other curriculum areas, students discover the connection between their current library literacy lessons and what they are being asked to accomplish in and out of school. Integrating skills into the classroom curriculum is beneficial to the students. Teaching for transfer is beneficial to students.

Neither flexible access nor flexible scheduling is necessary for the integration of skills or teaching for transfer to occur, but both facilitate and complement them. Of course, the integration of skills and teaching for transfer are school-wide goals and are not limited to library literacy lessons. Flexible access allows students to continue their learning in the library media center, and flexible scheduling allows integrated lessons to be taught in a timely manner.

When there is a listing of information literacy skills, it becomes easier to integrate them into library literacy lessons. If the students are able to immediately transfer their new skills to their classroom work, it strengthens their learning experiences. Library media specialists can enhance many already successful library literacy lessons and units by realigning them with appropriate classroom curriculum. They also can create new library media lessons to meet the students' skill needs. With the integration of skills, the library media specialist may need some suggestions for managing all the library literacy lessons. Integrating information literacy skills into the classroom curriculum and teaching for transfer to the students' school work help students learn more, remember more, and move faster toward becoming lifelong learners, readers, and library users.

TEACHING THE
ESSENTIAL LESSONS

Schools must teach certain subjects and lessons, as outlined by a curriculum. These are essential lessons and curriculum content. With an overall goal such as creating lifelong learners, readers, and library users, a school community will probably take another look at its list of essential lessons and curriculum content. Teaching students how to think and learn would be at the top of the list because the school is therefore preparing them for their lives after graduation, not just for their lives this semester. Howard County Public Schools in Maryland came to the realization that if every part of every curriculum was taught as outlined, the students would be in school for ten hours a day, maybe even more. The Howard County Board of Education then had teachers from each content area state succinctly what the "essential" goals were, then the process of integrating the curriculum goals was greatly simplified. In this way, two or more curriculums can be combined, while still satisfying the individual goals.

If the content area curriculums are streamlined to list only the essential skills, the library media curriculums must do the same. Old library media curriculums generally include literature appreciation, the location and use of materials, the production or creation of media, and becoming a lifelong reader. Newer library media curriculums added the evaluation and management of information, especially electronic information, and the goal of having students understand the ethical use of materials.

Today, library media skills have been regrouped, augmented, and renamed information literacy skills. Students' proficiency with information literacy skills is demonstrated rather than simply tested. Students are expected to reach certain levels of proficiency in these skills by certain grade levels.

Figure 7.1 includes two listings of information literacy skills, a generic list and AASL's. For students to succeed in any subject matter, they need these skills. If the students must locate print, nonprint, and electronic materials, efficiently and effectively that leads to library literacy lessons in the use of the catalog, finding videos on the shelves, accessing the Internet, and learning to use a table of contents, indexes, and so forth. Any of these library literacy lessons can be geared to first graders or to college students. A student's ability to use those library literacy skills builds on itself year after year, grade after grade.

Library Media and Information Literacy Skills

The student will be able to

- locate print, nonprint, and electronic materials efficiently and effectively

- select and evaluate materials critically and competently

- manage and use materials accurately and creatively

- appreciate materials and understand privacy and ethics in relation to materials

- understand the impact of technology on society

- create their own media and projects using technology

The American Association of
School Librarians' Information Literacy Skills

The basic elements of an information literacy curriculum:

I.   Defining the need for information
II.   Initiating the search strategy
III.   Locating the resources
IV.   Assessing and comprehending the information
V.   Interpreting the information
VI.   Communicating the information
VII.   Evaluating the product and process

Fig. 7.1. Some essential skills.

Information Power (American Association of School Librarians/Association for Educational Communications and Technology [AASL/AECT]) suggests that there are nine information literacy standards, and these are summarized into three overall categories: information literacy, independent learning, and social responsibility. These standards are listed on pages 8 and 9. The rest of Chapter 2 of *Information Power* contains ideas for integrating the standards into actual curriculum areas so that the principles can be met though the library media program. The three categories and nine principles are manageable and attainable.

In addition, the American Association of School Librarians (AASL) has a listing of information literacy skills in its position paper on information literacy that can be found on their Web site: http://www.ala.org/aasl/positions/ps_infolit.html (Information Literacy: A Position Paper on Information Problem Solving, ©1993 Copyright Wisconsin Educational Media Association). Figure 7.1 lists what AASL suggests are the seven basic foundations that should be considered and taught in information literacy curriculum. Each of the seven foundations lists further areas of accomplishment. The position paper also gives examples of information literacy skills integrated into classroom curriculums.

Various other educational groups have outlined what students should achieve. Succinctly, Howard County Public Schools (Howard County 1997) wants students to locate and retrieve, select and evaluate, organize and manage, comprehend and appreciate, and finally to create information. The Colorado information literacy standards (Colorado Department of Education 1999) want students to understand how to use and construct meaning from resources, produce and evaluate products, be self-directed and independent learners, participate in groups, and practice the ethical use of information. Montana's literacy guidelines (Montana Office of Public Instruction 1994) want students to be able to access information and use it, to be able to use various media, appreciate literature, and develop note-taking skills. Other school districts have adopted a listing of research skills. Some list five, six, or even nine steps that the students use. Many state departments of education have Web sites listing curriculum lessons. Listing the essential skills for classroom and library media curriculums is a way for school districts to create a broad outline of what should be included in their students' educational experiences.

LOOKING CLOSELY AT THE INTEGRATION OF SKILLS AND TEACHING FOR TRANSFER

The integration of the information literacy skills adds value to any lesson—be it a library literacy or classroom lesson—and increases the educational experiences of the students because they will be using those skills to complete classroom assignments. *Information Power* strongly supports the integration of skills. The first two principles of the "Learning and Teaching Principles of School Library Media Programs" are about integration. "Principle 1: The library media program is essential to learning and teaching and must be fully integrated into the curriculum to promote student's achievement of learning goals. Principle 2: The information literacy standards for student learning are integral to the content and objectives of the school's curriculum" (AASL/AECT 1998, p. 58). Both principles speak to having the information literacy skills integrated into the classroom curriculum through the library media program. The integration of these skills into the classroom curriculum is a great educational practice. Teaching for transfer is another great educational practice. Together, they teach the skills needed to accomplish a curriculum task at hand.

Information Literacy Skills Are
Easy to Integrate

Many library media specialists have been integrating information literacy skills into the classroom curriculum for years. Library literacy lessons are most easily connected with language arts, social studies, and science, but they also can be integrated into math, health, and other curriculums. One can accomplish this integration with or without planning or collaboration, but the benefits increase when the teacher is aware of what the library media specialist is teaching. Planning and collaboration with the teacher enables the lesson to be even more appropriate to the curriculum. As stated earlier, the integration of skills into the classroom curriculum can be done without flexible scheduling, although this system adds the dimension of the lesson occurring at the exact time that it is needed. There are many benefits to the integration of information literacy skills.

Donna P. Miller and J'Lynn Anderson (1994) pointed out that lessons integrated into the classroom curriculum help the students use those skills immediately, and hence they become more valuable. The authors also believe that this pushes the students to use higher-level thinking skills. Their book gives many examples of integrated lessons. The authors noted that flexible scheduling facilitates the integration of skills into lessons because the lessons can then be integrated into the classroom timeframe as well. Ms. Miller and Ms. Anderson have been very successful with their integrated library media center programs.

Two sets of lessons already described in this book provide examples of integrating information literacy skills into the classroom curriculum. One set of lessons is the one that creates the autobiographies for the first grade, as outlined in Chapters 2 and 4; the other is the creation of an atlas by the second grade, detailed in Chapter 2. Students learn about the parts of the book, and about other library media skills as well, by making a class biography book in first grade. They repeat the book-making process in second grade by making an atlas. Of course, the parts of a book are continuously mentioned during the year and perhaps reviewed in relation to a science, health, or language arts lesson. A library media specialist can refer to the student-produced books or even use the books as examples for other lessons concerning the parts of a book. Students put their knowledge of the parts of books to use. They know not only the parts of a book, but why they are included. What a difference it makes to be able to refer back to those lessons when the students are taught something related two or three years later. A lesson taught in isolation is easily forgotten. The aforementioned units taught students the parts of a book as they created their own classroom books. If a library media specialist teaches a lesson that focuses only on the parts of a book on a Wednesday from 10:00 to 10:30 a.m., the students wouldn't learn as much. They might learn that the parts of a book can be boring. But if students look up their name in the index of a book that their class made, they will be interested in using indexes. With the atlas lesson, students learn how to create a table of contents and how that process differs from the creation of an index. Creating the parts of a book with the students emphasizes the differences between table of contents and indexes. A table of contents and an index make sense and have a purpose for students—the purpose is for them to find their page or their map in the book to show their parents and friends. When skills are integrated into the classroom curriculum, students no longer look at the library media specialist quizzically to ask her why she would ever be teaching them something like this. Lessons have a purpose once they are integrated into the classroom curriculum, increasing their value in the eyes of the students.

It doesn't take a lot of planning to make the integration of information literacy skills happen. The fifth-grade team leader approached Pat Shrack, the library media specialist at Jeffers Hill Elementary School in Columbia, Maryland, to see if she would teach a lesson on note taking so that the students would be aware of different ways to take notes. The lead fifth-grade science teacher was standing nearby, so Mrs. Shrack asked what their next unit was going to be. When the teacher said it was ecosystems, the ideas started flowing. They developed plans for the fifth graders to learn note-taking skills in relation to their ecology unit during their library media times in the coming weeks. The lead science teacher informed the other teachers what was happening, and Mrs. Shrack adjusted a general note-taking lesson to reflect the needs of the students and the science unit as expressed by the science teacher. Through this one brief conversation, she took a first step toward the integration of skills into the classroom curriculum. Mrs. Shrack reinforced the students' educational experiences about note taking in a future lesson with camera techniques. Rather than expecting more work from the teacher, something was lifted from the teacher's workload. The students were ready to take notes in their science class. Further planning and collaboration to integrate skills with the fifth grade became a stronger possibility. Through integration, the library media specialist becomes the classroom teachers' ally and the classroom content lessons are reinforced by the library literacy lesson.

The integration of information literacy skills into the classroom curriculum isn't difficult when the library media specialist and teachers think ahead and can identify when two or more lessons can fit together to benefit the students. A library media specialist can decide what she wants the students to learn for the year and can start fitting the information literacy skills into the classroom curriculum. Teaching these skills creates information literate students. As the AASL Presidential Committee on Information Literacy stated, "Ultimately, information literate people are those who have learned how to learn. They know how to learn because they know how knowledge is organized, how to find information, and how to use information in such a way that others can learn from them. They are people prepared for lifelong learning, because they can always find the information needed for any task or decision at hand" (AASL Information Literacy Web page).

Teaching for Transfer Increases a Lesson's Worth

Many library media specialists realize that teaching for transfer adds a great deal to their lessons. Teaching for transfer occurs when students can apply what they've just learned to the lesson they're doing next. Teaching how to access the Internet to locate information about Washington, D.C., before the students take a trip there is teaching for transfer. Teaching for transfer is a bonus for any lesson.

Jean Donham van Deusen stated, "Cognitive theory tells us that to make learning meaningful, we need to associate learning in one setting with another, contextualize our learning, relate new learning to existing schemata and construct meaning for ourselves. When we give children isolated instruction unrelated to other intellectual events we leave the application of that instruction and the integration of it into other learning up to the child. Yet, what we know of transfer is that we must explicitly teach for transfer" (Donham van Deusen 1999, p. 224).

A lesson can include information literacy skills and yet not be taught for transfer. An old library media lesson about where materials are located might have found the students doing an exercise map here and a worksheet there, but not much else. Teach that same library media lesson integrated into a curriculum unit when the students' teacher says they need to come up with five reference resources for their big reports, and you'll see students wanting the lesson and putting their knowledge to use immediately. In this instance, the library media specialist has used the classroom curriculum to teach an information literacy lesson; at the same time, she reinforced what the teacher wants the students to do. The more the students know they need to learn certain things from more than one person, the better they will learn and retain that information. Follow that lesson about the selection of references with another assignment to select materials for the science fair, and teaching for transfer is occurring.

When those first and second graders who learned about the parts of a book reach the upper grades, opportunities will present themselves to expand on those lessons when literacy skills are taught. In the primary grades, the students created copyright dates, but now they have a chance to use the copyright dates in evaluating materials for their science fair projects. The copyright date they see now gives them information about the book. The copyright date can answer the question of, "Is this material up-to-date?" "Was it written after a big discovery?" "Should I use the information in it?" No longer is the student just saying, "The copyright date on my book is the year I was born!" but "The copyright date tells me there's a good chance that this book will have the information that I need." A review lesson concerning copyright dates is given as the students select books for their science projects. The library media specialist can point out other things that they already know about books—their location, the Dewey Decimal system, and more—and help students see how all their educational experiences interconnect and can be used in various situations with the assignments they have now—and even when they go to college.

Students are eager to learn new programs and put them to use. After learning how to use a drawing program and to print out a picture, they can put these skills to use immediately when next asked to produce a product for a content area project or when they illustrate a book or report they are writing. The lessons can include a comparison of drawing programs so that in the future, no matter what program they come across, they will be able to use it. The skill of knowing how to print and to operate printers on a network are also integrated into the drawing-program lesson. The library media specialist teaches the first lesson, but the classroom teacher will be able to follow up and help the students back in the classroom. They immediately transfer their new knowledge to their content area project, book, or report and will use this knowledge time and time again. The students learn a skill they will be able to use anytime, and it transfers to future learning experiences.

Many of these lessons begin to teach students how to learn no matter what the content is. Higher level and critical thinking skills are taught along with information literacy skills. Students are ready to apply these skills for various assignments and in various content areas. Simply said, students retain information best if they see the purpose for learning it and can use it right away.

Integrating information literacy skills, as well as teaching for transfer, increases a lesson's worth in the eyes of the students because their lessons are streamlined and their new knowledge can be put to use immediately. The students are on their way to becoming lifelong learners, readers, and library users because what they learn is meeting their needs as they occur.

ADJUSTING SUCCESSFUL LIBRARY LITERACY LESSONS

It is a challenge to take an old stand-alone lesson that is good and transform it into a lesson that is integrated into the classroom curriculum.

At a conference, while explaining that flexible scheduling can be at its best when it supports the integration of information literacy skills into the classroom curriculum, a fellow school library media specialist in attendance told me that she did not want to change what she taught. She had been teaching the same units for all these years, and students were expecting her units on puppets, folktales, photography, and the other units they had heard about from other students. The good news is that she doesn't really have to change what she teaches. She can still teach those units by adjusting them to match the curriculum.

It is a challenge, but a rewarding one, for a library media specialist to take stand-alone lessons and transform them into lessons that connect with the classroom curriculum, include student participation, and provide almost immediate utilization. Changing a lesson to connect with the curriculum is like braiding a French braid, making a model airplane, or using other Web sites to enhance a school Web page. A curriculum-related lesson has to be woven, arranged, glued, and connected to previous and future lessons. A library media specialist does not have to spend the summer overhauling all her lessons; in September opportunities will present themselves where she can change previous lessons as the year progresses. She can take a fresh look at previous lessons and turn a successful unit into an even more successful one when it is tied to what the students are doing in the classroom. Let's look at the units the conference attendee always taught and integrate her lessons with language arts, social studies, and science.

The creation of puppets can match any reading story from the language arts classroom curriculum. Characters can be developed, plot and story line discovered, and new endings easily created to extend the students' thinking. Students can create their own puppets and write their own stories that include their characters. There are many more ways to include puppets or puppet making into integrated lessons.

Folktales are easily integrated into the social studies curriculum. One of my favorite sets of lessons at Whiskey Bottom Road Elementary School was tying the Native American unit to the reading and creating of folktales. In an introductory lesson, I explained to the students that we would be creating their own folktales on filmstrips at the end of their classroom unit on Native Americans. I showed the filmstrip "How the Loon Got Its Necklace." Because the students were creating their own filmstrip, they needed to know what the Native Americans tribe ate and wore, how they lived, and so forth because these are, of course, interwoven into, if not the main idea, for a folktale. Throughout their unit, the students continued to read folktales and prepare to make their own filmstrips. Assignments were given, storyboards written, and all the facts that the teacher said they needed to know were interwoven into the original folktale.

A favorite of mine told why the river came to be. A young maiden was kidnapped and taken to the longhouse of another tribe. She cried and cried to be reunited with her people while dressed in her animal-skin clothing and eating venison, vegetables, and berries. A river forms from her tears, and her people cut down trees, make dugout canoes, and come to rescue her. If I remember that after all these years, I'm hopeful that the students will do as well. In this case we utilized flexible scheduling by scheduling extra classes throughout the unit so the library media center part of this unit ended at the same time as the social studies unit. Some students even worked at lunchtime to finish the filmstrips.

A lesson integrating historical fiction, biographies, and social studies is described in *School Library Activities Monthly*, February 1991 (Browne 1991). Again, students enjoyed this lesson, and it led them to use higher-level thinking skills by deciding how the characters could be in the same story and creating a story to connect them all. Integrating library literacy lessons into social studies units is a natural.

The library media specialist's photography lesson can be integrated with a science project of growing lima beans or other lessons in which experiments are involved. What a great time to teach the students how to use the digital camera and download their pictures and post them on an Internet site for their grandparents to see. When a lesson fits into the classroom curriculum, the ownership of that lesson is shared between the library media specialist and the classroom teacher. A photography lesson can be integrated into many subjects.

Integrating "old" library media lessons into the classroom curriculum is a challenge. Involving the students in their own learning is another challenge, and having them put their new knowledge to work immediately is an even greater challenge, yet the rewards are greater with each integration, involvement, and transfer.

CREATING NEW INTEGRATED LIBRARY LITERACY LESSONS

It may seem easier to start from scratch and create new library literacy lessons that integrate information literacy skills into the classroom curriculum, but it is still a challenge. The lesson or lessons can serve many purposes. It may need to fit into major school-wide units, match the school's curriculum, and teach the skills as well.

When starting from scratch, the library media specialist can suggest that the library literacy lessons serve as an introduction, a culminating lesson, or ongoing lessons in parallel with the class's lessons. Her involvement with the classroom lesson can range from just gathering materials for the classroom to teaching the majority of the unit. The library media specialist, teacher, or both decide those variables first. The library media specialist can teach the lesson or lessons alone or with the teacher, in the library media center or in the classroom. The new library literacy lessons have the opportunity to fulfill many purposes.

Some schools make it simpler for the library media specialist to integrate skills because they teach four major units a year and integrate all skills into those four units. Other school districts have adopted a framework, such as the "Big Six," "Habits of Mind," or "Six Traits Writing," that influences all they do in the district. Whether teaching school-wide units or utilizing a particular framework, the library media specialist may find it easier for to integrate the information literacy skills in these situations.

When library media specialists are creating new library media lessons, they may look at the curriculums used in their schools. Of course, the teachers decide when they are going to teach various units from the curriculum, and often they fill out a form for the school's administration, so that administrators will know what is taught and when. A library media specialist can access that curriculum form herself or ask the team leaders to fill out an abbreviated curriculum form quarterly.

Figure 7.2, on page 100, shows such a quarterly form that the fourth-grade team leader filled in. The library media specialist or administrators also can create a curriculum map, on which each subject's objectives are listed and developed for each grade level. *Developing an Integrated Library Program* (Miller and Anderson 1996) explains a curriculum map in more detail. Through whatever means, a library media specialist needs to know what students are learning and when.

Armed with information about what is to be taught in the classroom, the library media specialist can take a look at what she needs to teach to each grade for the year. The essential skills (Figure 7.1) should be spread throughout the year in a balanced way. The library media specialist can keep track of what is taught or needs to be taught for each grade level. A library media specialist should always reinforce previously taught library media lessons, as well as the classroom lessons. Having a general idea of what the teacher is covering and what skills the students need to be taught, a library media specialist may pick one curriculum content from Column A and one or two from skills Column B as in Figure 7.3, on page 100.

It helps if the library media specialist understands the objectives of the unit and the expectations for the students. It is also helpful to know if there are any specific new skills that the students will need to complete the unit. Chapter 8 outlines what is involved in planning with teachers.

Grade: 4		Team Leader: *Pam Jones*		Year: 2002
Subject \ Month	Math	Science	Social Science	Language Arts	Health
Feb.	*decimals fractions*	*electricity*	*colonial MD*	*write to persuade Fantasy*	*personal & consumer health*
Mar.	*graphing measurement division - 2 digit divisions*	*Force & motion*	*continued*	*continued*	*safety & first aid & injury prevention*
Apr.	*patterns, ratio, %, proportions*	*Earth Sc. geology*	*Revolutionary War*	*?*	*disease prevention control*

Fig. 7.2. A quarterly curriculum form.

Column A	**Column B**
Science	*Library media and technology skills*
electricity report	manage and create, locate resources
force and motion experiment	create, communicate information
geology field trip	appreciate and use, interpret information
Social studies	
Colonial Maryland reenactment	select and create; assess and comprehend information
Revolutionary War map	manage and create; locate, interpret, and communicate
Language arts	
fantasy authors	locate, initiate search strategy
write persuasive letters	evaluate; evaluate product and process
Health	
first aid chart	select; define need for information

Fig. 7.3. Pick from Column A and Column B.

Working with the teacher, a team, or by herself, the library media specialist can begin to plan a lesson or unit that will integrate the information literacy skills.

The suggestion for a new library literacy lesson might also come from a teacher. A third-grade teacher at Waterloo Elementary School asked me to help teach the students about the West Indies islands. The students would use the specialized series, *Lands and People*; they would use higher-level thinking and work with the information rather than just reproduce it; the students would write good informational paragraphs; and they would be creative by drawing a picture. All these skills were in one lesson when the students send their teacher a picture postcard telling about their pretend vacation on their island. Flexible scheduling helped with these lessons because we started with an hour lesson, quickly followed by two half-hour lessons to finish the postcards. The newly created lesson was a success.

When creating new lessons in which information literacy skills are taught, the library media specialist works with many variables. Her lesson may fit within a school's framework or she may have the opportunity to select various curriculum units to use as a backdrop for teaching skills. Creating new library literacy lessons gives the library media specialist a chance to demonstrate that the same skills can be taught with almost any content and materials to teach to the same ends. Each year it becomes progressively easier to integrate information literacy skills into the classroom curriculum.

USING HANDY LESSON LOGISTICS

If a school library media specialist is integrating information literacy skills into the classroom curriculum, she is busy. If she would like to keep her workday between the hours of 7:30 a.m. and 5:00 p.m., she needs lesson logistics that will help her manage the lessons.

First, it is easier to start the teaching week on Tuesday.

Second, librarian media specialists can place the materials for the library literacy lessons on a large table in the library media office or in baskets so that they can be gathered and are ready to use when needed.

Third, key words can be used to denote various library literacy lessons.

Fourth, the library media specialist can inform the rest of the school about what has been taught during a quarter.

Fifth, the same demonstration cards that depict spine labels and catalog entries can be used with every lesson.

Sixth, it is best, when planning a lesson, to start at the end of the lesson and plan backward to keep a lesson simple and straightforward.

Seventh, new materials can be the basis for the creation of new lessons.

Eighth, to keep track of individual students' performances during library literacy lessons, the library media specialist can use copies of her seating chart as a grade book.

Fig. 7.4. Handy lesson logistics.

First, it is easier to start the teaching week on Tuesday. If the library media specialist is teaching the same lesson for an entire grade level, she can plan that series of lessons to start on Tuesday and then have Monday to plan for the rest of the week. This was done with the fourth-grade historical fiction lesson shown in Figure 5.6.

Second, librarian media specialists can place the materials for the library literacy lessons on a large table in the library media office or in baskets so that they can be gathered and are ready to use when needed. When there are books, posters, or other hands-on materials, the table really comes in handy. The library media specialist also can start gathering for the next series of lessons and place those things on the table. This works well when there is a substitute library media specialist because everything is right there on the table.

Third, key words can be used to denote various library literacy lessons. These also can be used in the plan book, on the file folder where the lesson is kept, or on an envelope that holds the hands-on materials. Because there are many materials about the Dewey Decimal System, the library media specialist may need an envelope with all the Dewey picture cards, as well as a Dewey file folder with the overheads and lesson plan ideas in one folder. When she teaches a Dewey Decimal lesson, the word *Dewey* and a couple of key points can be written in the plan book to remind the library media specialist what she taught; she can place the actual lesson plan in the Dewey file folder, noting the grade and date it was taught. A little organization helps keep track of the many materials used with library literacy lessons.

Fourth, the library media specialist can inform the rest of the school about what has been taught during a quarter. A summary or list the lessons taught can be made for the teachers (see Figure 5.8, "Classes taught in the library"), and a quarterly report can be written for the administrators. At the end of the year, it is easy to provide a complete listing of the lessons taught that year, and that listing can be used as a guide for the following year. The listing also helps the library media specialist have an idea of what types of lesson have been taught.

Fifth, the same demonstration cards that depict spine labels and catalog entries can be used with every lesson. Over the years, the students see the same example cards. When fiction books are in the lesson, then the fiction card, complete with spine label and catalog entry, is shown to remind the students that "F" denotes a fiction book. Every year, the same cards are used for the same students.

Sixth, it is best, when planning a lesson, to start at the end of the lesson and plan backward to keep a lesson simple and straightforward. Are the students to use the information, locate the information, or simply know what kind of information is available? Those are three different lessons to be taught with encyclopedias. All three lessons cannot be done in one half-hour lesson. It helps to plan lessons carefully.

Seventh, new materials can be the basis for the creation of new lessons. New books, new equipment, new programs are easy to integrate into a lesson. These items can be used to add materials to the library media lessons.

Eighth, to keep track of individual students' performances during library literacy lessons, the library media specialist can use copies of her seating charts as a grade book. She can write directly on one of these charts noting the date, type, and subject of the lesson, as well as how each student did when reports or comments need to be made. The seating charts serve as a reminder of past performance.

Other library media specialists may have many more suggestions about teaching, organizing materials, and settling into a comfortable pattern. No matter what, the library media specialist will have opportunities to try fresh ideas when managing library literacy lessons.

The desire to integrate information literacy skills into the classroom curriculum is what started flexible scheduling. With the integration of information literacy skills, the library media specialist is no longer teaching in isolation, and the students enjoy the advantage of having their learning experiences connected with their classroom curriculum. Whether a library media specialist is adjusting successful library literacy lessons or creating new ones, all of the work that goes into these lessons helps create lifelong learners, readers, and library users. Integrating library literacy lessons into the classroom curriculum is one of the greatest things that can be done for the students, teachers, and for the library media specialist.

Chapter 8

PLANNING AND COLLABORATING WITH TEACHERS

Around the conference table at the Afternoon School, those guiding the changes being made at the school are discussing the benefits of having more collaboration among the teaching staff, among themselves, and in particular with the library media specialist, as they do at the Day School.

> *We are on our way to becoming a Day School.*
> *We're on our way to creating lifelong learners, readers, and library users especially because we've agreed to integrate the information literacy skills into the classroom curriculum and to be aware of teaching for transfer.*
> *Now we need to be working toward getting the teachers to plan with each other and with the library media specialist—and ultimately to collaborate—because collaboration facilitates our goal of creating lifelong learners, readers, and library users, just as flexible access and scheduling help a school reach that goal.*
> *I know they collaborate at the Day School. We want to collaborate, too!*

If the Afternoon School wants to be like the Day School, it must progress from casual planning to full-fledged collaboration. A great school is one in which everyone works together toward the same long-term goal—collaborating. The library media specialist's leadership and the expectation of the principal that planning takes place will make collaboration happen. Making use of collaboration will move a school forward to create lifelong learners, readers, and library users. A school that collaborates is a stronger school.

Information Power also discusses collaboration. Principles 3 and 4 of the "Learning and Teaching Principles of School Library Media Programs" state how the library media program should relate to collaboration. Principle 3 states, "The library media program models and promotes collaborative planning and curriculum development (and) Principle 4: The library media program models and promotes creative, effective, and collaborative teaching" (American Association of School Librarians and Association for Educational Communications and Technology [AASL/AECT] 1998, p. 58). *Information Power* then outlines goals for the library media specialist in relationship to collaboration and discusses how these principles can be acted out.

Announcing that "Starting tomorrow, because we now have flexible scheduling, there will be 30 minutes of planning time each week between teachers and the library media specialist," is not the way to introduce planning and collaboration. Teachers will be concerned that planning with the library media specialist will take up more time, and then they'll be unsure what role the library media specialist will take, let alone what the usual role of the library media specialist is. A staff usually figures that any change will mean more work for them, and they have too much to do now. They might even be unsure how it would be to work together with the library media specialist or perhaps even other team members because many teachers have always worked on their own. This sentiment is echoed time and time again in articles about flexible scheduling—teachers are reluctant to plan with the library media specialist. Of course, library media specialists are happy to plan with teachers so that they will no longer be isolated in their teaching. Planning in isolation isn't as productive as planning together or collaborating with staff.

There is a recognizable progression from planning to collaboration. The planning or cooperation that develops first between planning team members is short term, informal, structureless, and doesn't feel risky to the participants, for their roles remain the same. The next step is coordination between the participants when they work within a longer timeframe and start on an understood mission. The coordinating participants' relationships are more formal, and a "boss" may surface after some discussion. Collaboration among participants is for the long term. Collaborative relationships are created and strengthen as comprehensive planning occurs. The progression from casual planning to collaboration can be made smoothly when the participants know that everyone understands it takes time to form collaborative relationships.

The library media specialist's role on a collaborative team is strengthened if the principal supports the library media specialist in fulfilling the designated roles of instructional consultant to the staff, a teaching partner, the manager of the library resources, and a teacher of all students. The principal's support greatly facilitates the move from casual planning to full-fledged collaboration. Julie I. Tallman and Jean Donham van Deusen explained the importance of the support of the school's administration: "principals who expected teacher/library media specialist collaboration had media programs that were more than ancillary. This underscores the importance of principals having an understanding of the benefits of collaboration between teachers and library media specialists" (Tallman and Donham van Deusen 1995, p. 204). When collaborative planning is tied into the overall school-wide goals, its implementation will be successful.

Neither flexible access nor flexible scheduling are necessary for collaboration between the teachers and the library media specialist, but these concepts facilitate, highlight, and support collaboration because they allow the use of the library media center, its resources, and its services at times deemed necessary by the collaborative planning. If a teacher decides that a small group should gather information for the whole class, flexible access allows that to happen; flexible scheduling allows for relevant lessons to be taught in a timely manner, based on the classroom's schedule, that has been jointly planned. Both flexible access and flexible scheduling offer options that would not be available with a fixed library media center schedule.

Let's look at some suggestions that start a school's library media specialist on the road toward collaboration. The library media specialist should do some preplanning by himself, create the useful plan book as outlined in Chapter 5, adjust to the teacher's planning styles, and start the planning process at a comfortable level for himself and the staff. Through all of these situations, the library media specialist will try to make his schedule workable. There are many books and articles available on the planning process and on collaboration. A school can be successful as long as it is continually moving forward toward collaboration with principal support and encouragement.

PREPLANNING

A library media specialist is well prepared to plan with teachers if he does some preplanning during the summer. Preplanning starts with a year's calendar on which all the holidays, quarters and semesters, testing and conferences, and other major events are blocked out on the calendar. With those blocked out, the library media specialist and others can see the actual time that is available for teaching—short weeks, broken-up weeks, three full weeks in a row, and so forth. The library media lessons and school's curriculum must fit around this calendar, and by looking ahead, anyone can get an idea how much real teaching time is available. As an example, a production unit might fit well before the holidays, when there are three full weeks of school in a row, and maybe the three-week reference materials unit would fit in second semester just before testing begins. A yearly calendar is not only helpful for the library media specialist, but for the whole school.

Because the school's curriculum guides library media lessons, the library media specialist writes down what happened the year before and what could and should happen in the coming school year. Anything that was postponed from the last year is automatically added to this year's list of lessons so that it is not missed again. By the middle of August, the library media specialist will have, in mind or on paper, what will be taught for each grade that year. Some topics may include orientation, search strategies, relevant reference materials, production of media, interpretation of materials, appreciation and location of print, nonprint, and electronic materials, as well as all the other information literacy skills (see Chapter 7).

With a calendar and an outline of the classroom and library literacy curriculum, the library media specialist will have a "big picture" in mind when he starts planning with the teachers. He can share this overview with the teachers, not to dictate what will take place and when, but to provide a framework for the planning. Getting a feel for how the calendar and the curriculum can fit together for the school year helps the library media specialist preplan for the year.

× = No School
○ = No Students
— = ½ Day Kids
△ = Report Cards
□ = Testing

AUGUST

S	M	T	W	T	F	S
		1	2	3	4	5
6	7	8	9	10	11	12
13	14	15	16	(17)	(18)	19
20	(21)	(22)	(23)	24	25	26
27	28	29	30	31		

SEPTEMBER

S	M	T	W	T	F	S
					1	2
3	✕	5	6	7	8	9
10	11	12	13	14	15	16
17	✕	19	20	21	22	23
24	25	26	27	28	29	30

OCTOBER

S	M	T	W	T	F	S
1	2	3	4	5	6	7
8	9	10	11	12	13	14
15	16	17	18	19	20	21
22	23	24	25	26	✕	28
29	30	31				

NOVEMBER

S	M	T	W	T	F	S
			1	2	3̶	4
5	(6)	(7)	8	/9\	10	11
12	13	14	15	16̶	17̶	18
19	20	21	22	23	24	25
26	27	28	29	✕		

DECEMBER

S	M	T	W	T	F	S
					✕	2
3	4	5	6	7	8	9
10	11	12	13	14	15	16
17	18	19	20	21	22	23
24	✕	✕	✕	✕	✕	30
31						

JANUARY

S	M	T	W	T	F	S
	✕	✕	3	4	5	6
7	8	9	10	11	12	13
14	15	16	17	18	1̶9̶	20
21	✕	23	24	25	/26\	27
28	29	30	31			

FEBRUARY

S	M	T	W	T	F	S
				1	2	3
4	5	6	7	8	9	10
11	12	13	14	15	16	17
18	✕	20	21	22	23	24
25	26	27	28			

MARCH

S	M	T	W	T	F	S
				1	2	3
4	5	6	7	8	9	10
11	12	13	14	15	16	17
18	[19]	[20]	[21]	[22]	[23]	24
25	26	27	28	2̶9̶	✕	31

APRIL

S	M	T	W	T	F	S
1	✕	✕	✕	✕	✕	7
8	9	10	11	12	/13\	14
15	16	17	1̶8̶	1̶9̶	(20)	21
22	(23)	24	25	26	27	28
29	30					

MAY

S	M	T	W	T	F	S
		1	2	3	4	5
6	[7]	[8]	[9]	[10]	[11]	12
13	[14]	[15]	[16]	[17]	[18]	19
20	21	22	23	24	25	26
27	✕	29	30	31		

JUNE

S	M	T	W	T	F	S
					1	2
3	4	5	6	7̶	/8\	9
10	11	12	13	14	15	16
17	18	19	20	21	22	23
24	25	26	27	28	29	30

Fig. 8.1. A school's yearly calendar.

ADJUSTING STEPS IN THE PLANNING PROCESS

For some teachers, sharing their plan book with the library media specialist is like opening their checkbook to an Internal Revenue Service agent. Can they trust the library media specialist to see only the positive in their scribbles or blank pages? A library media specialist keeps many planning fundamentals in mind while he plans with teachers and starts the process of building a good level of trust with each staff member.

First, it is a complicated process to plan with others.

Second, there are different types of planning.

Third, many planning guides have been developed over the years.

Fourth, planning can take place at any time, but the best time to plan is when the teacher or teachers are available.

Fifth, planning time can be made productive and enjoyable.

Fig. 8.2. Planning fundamentals.

First, it is a complicated process to plan with others. Linda Lachance Wolcott wrote an excellent article for *School Library Media Quarterly*, "Understanding How Teachers Plan" in the spring of 1994. She said, "Planning instruction is an activity in which all teachers engage but few may articulate or reflect upon" (Wolcott 1994, p. 162). When the library media specialist comes along and says, "Let's plan together," teachers may be reluctant. They may be comfortable with their own planning but totally unsure about planning with others. Planning is "both a psychology process and a practical activity" (Wolcott 1994, p. 162). A library media specialist may be uncomfortable planning with others as well. As the library media specialist approaches planning with the teachers, he keeps in mind that the process is complicated and that each person plans differently.

Second, there are different types of planning. Ms. Wolcott explained that teachers plan for different reasons: to satisfy psychological needs, to prepare themselves and the lesson, to create a framework, or because they are required to do so. There also are different types of planning: hourly, weekly, daily, unit, and long range. Some teachers plan incrementally for the short term, others for the long term. The planning process seems to be a cyclical process, not a linear one, so it many not be easy to record or share with someone else. The library media specialist needs to take all of this information into consideration as he approaches each teacher or planning team.

Third, many planning guides have been developed over the years. They are good points of departure to make sure everything that needs to be is covered. A school also may develop their own. Notes need to be taken during the planning process so that the planners can go back over details this year and in the future. Like flexible access and flexible scheduling, the planning process is a means to an end, not an end in itself so the paperwork for the planning process should be kept simple. If a school's administrators, the library media specialist, or the teachers need a formal record of the planning accomplished, they can create one like that in Figure 8.3.

Planning Guide for Teaching Partners	Activities and products:	Planned lessons (cont.):
Curriculum area: _____ Unit of study: _____ Unit time length: _____ Beginning on: _____ Periods curriculum is taught: _____ _____ Best teaching times: _____ _____ Teachers involved: _____ _____	Resources:	Evaluation:
Goals and Objectives:	Responsibilities:	Next Planning Mtg.: _____ Results and adjustments for next year:
Student Outcomes/Skills:	Planned lessons:	

Fig. 8.3. One example of a planning guide.

Somewhere in the planning process, the overall goal or goals of the lesson is noted, along with specific objectives, concepts, and skills to be learned from the various curriculum areas. These can be ranked in order of importance after the teachers share the student's current competency levels. The library media specialist may know if the students have the prerequisite knowledge for the lesson, or he may need to gather this information from the teacher. The library media specialist might even wish to note any strong student learning styles because they would affect the way the lessons are taught. It's best to note how the students will gather, record, process, or organize the information to be taught and how the students will create a product of their findings. Guided practice and active learning should be included to heighten the amount of information that will be retained, as well as to look at the lesson from the point of view of teaching for transfer. Independent practice also might be given to facilitate independent learning. As the library media specialist starts to gather resources and prepare for the lesson, some of these steps may be adjusted. Last but not least, an outline of how to evaluate the projects and work is developed. In this process, the various responsibilities the teacher carries out are listed for both the teacher and the library media specialist, and perhaps other teachers, noting timeframe. If the planning notes are not clearly written, should be unscrambled after meeting so that the ideas are not lost. Any tie-in lessons can be planned at a future session. Figure 8.3 gets that information on one side of a piece of paper. Other planning guides are available in (Buchanan 1991, Loertscher 1988, Montana Office of Public Instruction 1994, Page 1999, and Zweizig and McAfee Hopkins 1999).

After the lessons have been taught, the planning team should make an assessment of the lessons to note what changes should be made for the next year. At the same time, the team can create a list of resources for the next year, remembering that the Library Power experience demonstrates that having adequate and up-to-date materials to help teach the curriculum units is a positive influence that moves a school toward collaboration. When the planning process is just beginning, the use of a planning guide is helpful, almost necessary, if planning is to be efficient.

Fourth, planning can take place at any time, but the best time to plan is when the teacher or teachers are available. Many times, the library media specialist is teaching during a teacher's scheduled planning time, so most joint planning with the library media specialist takes place before or after school—usually within the stated contract hours. Planning with all grade levels in one week is overwhelming. The library media specialist has to plan with all of them at the beginning of the year but can then spread out the process so he isn't in meetings all week. A group can plan a natural amount of lessons in advance, maybe four or six weeks ahead, planning through a report card or exam time and through holidays. No one wants to plan on the first day back from vacation. Most important, it is hoped that the library media specialist can always say "yes" when asked to plan with the teachers. Initially, it is important for the library media specialist to be flexible with the teachers' schedule because he is asking them to be so with his. It is hoped that with most grade levels, the library media specialist will be able to plan monthly, or as needed, but will not require a dictated set schedule to accomplish the tasks at hand. Setting a fixed planning time negates the flexibility the school is seeking. Planning times are best scheduled as needed. When the library media specialist has taught most of the planned library literacy lessons, he can remind the teaching team that it is time to plan more lessons. It is best to plan flexibly on the teachers' schedule.

Fifth, planning time can be made productive and enjoyable. Because the library media specialist wants to make planning a positive experience, he should be on time, bring ideas, be willing to brainstorm, and bring treats. At planning meetings, the library media specialist presents himself as wanting to help the teachers provide information that students need to know to succeed with the teacher's lesson. As discussed in Chapter 7, the library media specialist can give an introductory lesson, a concluding lesson, a production lesson, an information-gathering lesson, or a skill lesson. The planning team can meet in a classroom, where the library media specialist sees what items are on the walls and what materials are using for the lesson, or it can meet in the library media center to see the resources there.

If someone raises the issue that planning with the library media specialist will mean extra planning for the teachers, the library media specialist suggests that including him in the planning process might mean a change in planning time, but overall the amount of planning time needed will not increase by much. In fact, it may even decrease, given that more people are now available to locate materials, plan, and teach the lessons. Everyone will be pleased if the whole process is kept as short and simple as possible. Planning can be a exciting, positive time.

STARTING THE PLANNING PROCESS AT A COMFORTABLE LEVEL

A library media specialist is disturbed when she hears the following remarks coming from classrooms as he walks down the hall:

> *Now class, today we start our unit on the Egyptians. Use the library media center, and I'll want a two-page report from each of you in two weeks.*
>
> ** * **
>
> *Class, we don't have many materials in the classroom about inventions. I wish we did, but you can go to the public library and see what they have.*

Hearing either one of those statements starts a library media specialist talking to himself.

> *How can "they" do this? At the last faculty meeting, I explained that I wanted to be involved in planning units and sharing resources! Has anyone been listening?! I wrote a whole pamphlet on library media services!*

Well, maybe those two teachers were listening and reading, but they still may not know what to do or where to start. Given these situations, the library media specialist needs to make an opportunity to speak to these two teachers casually and make just one, maybe two, suggestions as to how the library media center might be able to help their students complete the assignments.

The library media specialist can do much more, but at the beginning stages of collaborative planning, putting forth just a few of the suggestions is a good start. If they are hooked into the library media center on this project, the library media specialist can suggest more on the next project.

Starting with casual planning and building to collaboration is similar to using an interior decorator. If the homeowner wants to add some accent pieces here and there to pull a room together, but ends up with the interior decorator suggesting that a wall should be torn out, a new couch purchased, and wooden floors installed, the homeowner will be overwhelmed, not pleased. When a library media specialist plans with teachers, he can initially start with the accent pieces and move slowly to the new couch. The principal is in charge of tearing down the walls.

The whole planning process can be kept in perspective if the library media specialist keeps the following in mind:

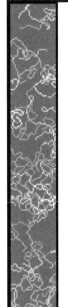

First, it's easy for the library media specialist to start with casual planning.

Second, planning notes for teachers can simplify the planning process.

Third, the library media specialist can start planning with just one teacher.

Fourth, team planning and team collaboration is the ultimate goal for the school.

Fifth, the library media specialist can be involved with the classroom curriculum lessons at many levels.

Sixth, planning is a balancing act for everyone.

Seventh, scheduling the library literacy lessons in the library media specialist's plan book is truly a balancing act.

Eighth, smart teachers learn to plan early.

Fig. 8.4. Planning suggestions.

First, it's easy for the library media specialist to start with casual planning. When teachers are in the hall or while coming or going from the faculty lounge, he can start the process of planning. If the teacher takes the bait, then he can meet with the teacher with a piece of paper and plan book in hand to write things down and finalize the process. Mrs. Shrack's note-taking lesson described in Chapter 7 is a good example of casual planning. Casual planning can occur at any time, but it is not the best idea to try and plan over lunch. Both teachers and library media specialists need time to talk about other things during the day. Casual planning can be the start for collaborative planning.

Second, planning notes for teachers can simplify the planning process. A library media specialist can start the planning process by placing a short note in a teacher's mailbox to make a suggestion for a library literacy lesson on the topic that is coming up. The teacher can read the idea at her leisure (see Figure 8.5 on page 114).

Dear Elaine,

It would be great to introduce Dr. Seuss to your students. I'd show pictures, show most of his books, and a fast-moving filmstrip that covers his life. Then I'd like to share one of his books that you haven't read with the kids.

What have you read?

_____

_____

I'm available these times. Circle your best time:

Mon.   9/21   1:00   1:30
Wed.   9/23   1:30   2:00
Thurs.   9/24   1:00

The lesson would take 30 minutes. I'd be happy to share my materials with you. Would you like the "Cat in the Hat" doll for your classroom for the next two weeks?

Fig. 8.5. A planning note to a first-grade teacher.

This note to Elaine on library media notepaper gives her options as to scope and times of the lessons and allows her to make easy decisions. When the note comes back, the library media specialist may simply need to touch base to say, "Thank you, see you next week." It is always prudent to make a copy of any note so one can send it again if it gets lost. Planning by notes gives the teacher and library media specialist a little more time to digest what is being asked and what times are available.

Third, the library media specialist can start planning with just one teacher. Setting a time to sit down with just one teacher from a team and look over the next couple of weeks or a month to see what can be done is one way to start planning with teachers. Plan a lesson with a teacher's or library media specialist's favorite unit or with the teacher's least favorite lesson as discussed in Chapter 4. Social studies units seem to be the easiest to integrate, but perhaps the most involved. If the library literacy lesson is successful, then the library media specialist tells the other teachers of that grade level about it, suggesting that the same lesson be taught to their students. Then everyone need only agree on a time for the library literacy lesson. The teachers with whom the library media specialist has planned become advocates among their colleagues for the library media center. Perhaps the planning for that one teacher is extended to all the teachers on the team without their being involved in the process. When that lesson is a success, others are more willing to try planning with the library media specialist.

Librarian Becky Roesch from McClave, Colorado, wrote to me that "successful flexible scheduling is often a result of successful fixed scheduling." If the teacher likes the lesson you conduct with the class at their usual time, perhaps the teacher will want to spread the lessons into other subjects, which might necessitate flexible scheduling. With each successful lesson and interaction, the library media specialist is building a solid base from which to work in the future.

Fourth, team planning and team collaboration is the ultimate goal for the school. To get team planning started, the library media specialist speaks or sends a note to the team leader or chair suggesting that planning needs to take place. With team planning, everyone, whole teams and resource people, who is involved plans together. It is important to remember to include resource and special-education teachers in the planning process. The whole grade level or particular subject is discussed, and overall plans are made for a month or six weeks. Putting in specific times for each class to be taught the lesson can be done later, individually. A single note can get the planning process started.

Marilyn Oswald of Austin, Minnesota, told me that "There are all kinds of teachers and all kinds of teaching styles. Take the time to get to know your teachers well. To plan a successful activity, you have to know when to lead, when to follow, and when to compromise. The classroom teacher needs to get comfortable with each of the roles you and he/she has. The classroom teacher also has to feel that the activity planned is valuable and worth the time invested." Planning is a process that leads to collaboration when there is comprehensive planning with everyone involved.

Fifth, the library media specialist can be involved with the classroom curriculum lessons at many levels. He can start by getting involved in the classroom teacher's lesson on a simple level, such as having a class come in to locate the materials they might need for their papers and place those on a reserve cart for their use. On the next level, the teacher might introduce the lesson in the classroom, and then the library media specialist helps the students prepare a bibliography, taking notes, and using the Internet. A library media specialist will be more involved with the lesson if he and the teacher teach the students how to decide which material is truly useful and how to create new information from what they have researched. Later, the library media specialist might be the lead teacher for the whole curriculum unit. It is wonderful when he and the teacher go back and forth as lead teacher during the lesson. At this point, teachers begin to see that collaboration does not mean more work for them, but work of a different kind that is more rewarding without being more time-consuming. A library media specialist can be involved with the classroom lessons on various levels.

Sixth, planning is a balancing act for everyone. In the planning process, the participants want to come to a consensus. Each planning team member needs to have a feel for how the planning is going and add more or fewer suggestions. When planning, the team leader usually starts by telling the planning team what the grade level will be doing for the next month or so. Everyone can brainstorm to come up with various ideas to integrate information literacy skills into the general curriculum. The library media specialist also can think of the library literacy lessons done last year for this unit, what information literacy skills still need to be taught, and whether this unit lends itself to the production of a final product. As the planning session ends, the library media specialist will want to leave with a listing of expected outcomes, a possible if not a firm timeframe for the lessons, and any teacher-produced handouts, forms, or resources. The planning guides mentioned earlier help to streamline the planning process. The library media specialist will leave with enough information about the lessons to start planning for them. Planning is a give-and-take process.

Seventh, scheduling the library literacy lessons in the library media specialist's plan book is truly a balancing act. I presented various examples of library media schedules in Chapters 4 and 5. When setting library literacy lesson times with the teacher, the library media specialist should have some ideas as to what times would work for everyone, and he should be prepared to share those. If a teacher prefers to hold the lesson back-to-back with a special, the library media specialist can accommodate that request, saying he hopes there will be an opportunity to have a library literacy lesson during the actual curriculum time. In Figure 5.6, two of the fourth-grade lessons on historical fiction are taught back-to-back with a special, the other two are taught during the language arts times, and all four lessons are taught in one day. That scheduling makes the day a little stressful for the library media specialist but serves the purpose of having all classes introduced to historical fiction in one day given the class times available. Also, teachers are asked to respond to many scheduling and curriculum demands, so scheduling a library literacy lesson may not be as high a priority for them as it is for the library media specialist. Other library media lessons in Figure 5.6 also were taught back-to-back with the class's special, but the second-grade library literacy lesson was the social studies lesson and had to be taught between 2:00 and 3:00 p.m. As the library media specialist works with a flexible schedule, he will begin to understand that there are many possible library literacy lesson times, and he can guide the selection of the best and most convenient ones for everyone involved.

Eighth, smart teachers learn to plan early. Eventually some teachers realize that if they plan with the library media specialist early, they will have more possible lesson times from which to choose. Smart teachers also figure out that the library media specialist is a valuable resource. They come to him for assistance even when lessons are not involved. There are always a few teachers who understand the planning process extremely well.

Starting to plan and share teaching responsibilities with one teacher, then with a team, and finally with the whole school can take a while, but it is beneficial for everyone—students, teachers, and the library media specialist. *Information Power* lists and discusses good suggestions for collaborating (AASL/AECT 1998, Chapter 2, "Collaboration, Leadership and Technology"). If a school wishes to move toward collaborative planning, they can start at a comfortable level and move toward full collaboration.

Through planning, coordination, cooperation, and collaboration, the whole school starts to work as one team. The principal's expectations are important, as is the library media specialist's leadership, to move a school toward collaboration. Collaboration is one of the best means to move students ahead in their educational experiences. Planning with teachers may be a challenge for a library media specialist, but the gains are great for all. It makes sense to continually pursue a goal of collaboration. When staff members are team players, the whole school grows. Collaboration among school community members creates lifelong learners, readers, and library users.

Chapter 9

SHARING THE ADVANTAGES OF FLEXIBLE ACCESS AND FLEXIBLE SCHEDULING WITH THE SCHOOL COMMUNITY

I f the Afternoon School wants to be like the Day School, it needs the support of the whole school community, those in the school building (students, teachers, and staff) and those in the larger community who are affiliated with the school (parents, board of education personnel, local government officials, business owners, and the general public). All of these people play a role in the education of a school's students. The school library media center and library media specialist also play an important role in educating students, but just as the implementation of flexible access and flexible scheduling are not necessary to having an integrated resource-based curriculum and a collaborating staff, students could be educated having only a fixed library media schedule as they do at the Night School. That could happen, but the students certainly wouldn't be as well educated as they are at the Day School, where they can truly become lifelong learners, readers, and library users. Integrating skills, teaching for transfer, using a resource-based curriculum, and having a staff that collaborates, as well as flexible access and flexible scheduling, are the key to a win-win situation for a school community. Flexible access and flexible scheduling facilitate, highlight, and support all educational changes, reforms, and goals.

Whether a school community's goal is to create lifelong learners, readers, and library users; to raise students' test scores; or to do something else, flexible access and flexible scheduling have their advantages. Facts and figures are available to share with the school's community that support flexible access and scheduling, and they both offer additional advantages. Sharing the pluses of flexible access and flexible scheduling with the school community provides an opportunity to highlight the overall value of the library media center and the library media specialist. Naturally, there are challenges that flexible access and flexible scheduling present, but one can meet them by gathering feedback and making adjustments to suit the school.

The Afternoon School team that is directing the changes in their school are discussing some of the facts, figures, and benefits of flexible access and flexible scheduling that they'll present to the rest of the school community.

We need to present to our school community some facts and figures about flexible access and flexible scheduling.

The Library Power program gives us some examples and percentages we can share.

Are they good numbers?

When principals, teachers, and library media specialists are asked if both concepts should continue in the schools, most responses are in the 90-percent range.

What about that Colorado study?

Yes, the Library Research Services did more studies. In Colorado in particular, it found that when a school allowed flexible access to the library, it was an indicator that it would have higher academic achievement than a school that did not. Other services provided by the library media center were also indicators of higher academic achievement.

Any other information to share with our school community members?

Well, flexible access and flexible scheduling sound so logical when their advantages are outlined that surely people will be able to see and hear the positive aspects of both concepts.

Remembering what we've learned about change, I think we need to share our vision of what our students can achieve. Let's explain how we'll proceed, present the few adjustments that need to be made, ask for feedback, and outline the benefits of the educational changes we wish to make in our school.

That sounds like a good plan. Remember flexible access and flexible scheduling fit right in with the educational changes we want to make in our school. We truly want to create lifelong learners, readers, and library users.

We want to be like the Day School.

RECOGNIZING WHAT
FLEXIBLE ACCESS OFFERS

There are many advantages to instituting flexible access in a school because this concept is about providing students with opportunities to visit and use the library media center, its resources, and its services. In reality, students must be allowed to use the library media center before they would ever become a lifelong library user, let alone a learner and reader. The Library Power programs (Zweizig and McAfee Hopkins 1999), as well as the recent Colorado study by the Library Research Service (Lance, Rodney, and Hamilton-Pennell 2000), provides us with facts and figures that offer actual and perceived advantages of flexible access. The additional advantages are created as a result of instituting various aspects of flexible access. Every advantage of flexible access generates a positive thrust on which the school community can move to improve the way it educates students.

Facts and Figures Agree:
There Are Advantages to Flexible Access

When circulation figures rise and the number of visits to the library media center increases, something good is happening. The Library Power program collected figures throughout the timeframe of the program at the various schools so these comparisons could be made. The Colorado study measured indicators of higher student achievement through the correlation of various pieces of information. Both studies have generated some information that we can share with the school community, especially the administrators of the school.

According to Zweizig and McAfee Hopkins, "Students in 95 percent of the Library Power schools have flexible or semiflexible access to their library media center using the center on an average of one and a half times a week as an individual, a member of a class or a small group" (American Association of School Librarians, *Information Power,* p. 140). Further figures that are reported in *Lessons from Library Power* (Zweizig and McAfee Hopkins 1999) and shown in Figure 9.1 indicate that students in the Library Power schools use of the library media center improved, that individual students used it much more often than before, and that students had a much more positive attitude toward using it. As noted in Figure 9.1, library media specialists, principals, and teachers agreed that on-demand use of the library media center should and would continue in most Library Power schools (Zweizig and McAfee Hopkins 1999).

In the Library Power Schools where there is flexible access and flexible scheduling (Zweizig and McAffee Hopkins 1999, pp. 49–50):

Student Frequency of Using the Library
      32.5% said they used the library "more than before" flexible access
      32.3% said "much more than before"

Student Frequency of Using the Library on Their Own Initiative
      32.1% said "more often"
      27.9% said "much more often"

Student Attitude Toward Using the Library
      32.1% said "more positive"
      39.6% said "much more positive"

When librarians, principals, and teachers were asked if flexible access *will* continue
      93.2% of the librarian said "yes"
      96.9% of the principals said "yes"
      90.7% of the teachers said "yes"

When librarians, principals, and teachers were asked if flexible access *should* continue
      97.0% of the librarian said "yes"
      98.0% of the principals said "yes"
      90.0% of the teachers said "yes"

Fig. 9.1. Facts and figures for flexible access.

The latest Colorado Study (Lance, Rodney, and Hamilton-Pennell 2000) findings link flexibly accessed library programs with higher levels of academic achievement. Hearing Keith Curry Lance explain these results at the Colorado Educational Media Association (CEMA) annual conference (February 19, 2000), it was understood that they had in fact measured flexible access to the library media center, and not flexible scheduling as we are defining it in this book. Lance and others at Library Research Service found that "When access to library media centers is scheduled [accessed] flexibly, reading scores improve 13 to 22 percent. Flexible scheduling [access] allows students to visit the LMC individually" (Lance, Rodney, and Hamilton-Pennell 2000, p. 2). Those results certainly seem in line with the idea that if a school allows students access to the library media center when they need resources and information, it is more likely to value lifelong learning, reading, and library use. A school like that would naturally have higher test scores than would one that does not allow students to use the library media center. Flexible access encourages student achievement. These figures are helpful when convincing others in the school community to embrace flexible access.

There Are Additional Advantages to Flexible Access

There are even more advantages to instituting flexible access. These begin to appear as the school allows more access to the library media center, its resources, and its services. Chapters 2, 4, and 5 outline the variables of flexible access that are reviewed as advantages in the present chapter. The advantages derived from having flexible access to the library media center can be shared with a school community.

First, flexible access strengthens a school community's support of the library media center.

Second, the library media space is better and more fully utilized with flexible access.

Third, flexible access maximizes the use of the resources in the library media center.

Fourth, flexible access changes the way students are educated when the library media center becomes an annex to the classroom.

Fifth, flexible access encourages and helps patrons of the larger school community continue or become lifelong learners, readers, and library users when a school extends the library media center's services beyond its walls.

Sixth, patrons misplace or lose fewer library media center books when they can return and check out materials at anytime.

Seventh, flexible access promotes self-directed and self-paced learning.

Fig. 9.2. Advantages to having flexible access.

First, flexible access strengthens a school community's support of the library media center. When the library media center is filled with learners, administrative and school-community support for flexible access begins to grow. When instituting even a small degree of flexible access, the results can be noticeable. Some students will go in and out of the library media center as often as they can. Any flexible access to the library media center usually gathers support not only for flexible access, but also for the library media program. Parents appreciate the fact that their student can check out a book at almost any time. When there is a library media center filled with learners because it is open to them, the results will be positive, and support for the library media center and its program will strengthen.

Second, the library media space is better and more fully utilized with flexible access. A little rearranging and some encouragement of the teachers may be all that a school needs to do to make strides toward creating a busy library media center. Rather than only five classes of twenty-five students using the library media center in a day, it could be used by as many as ten classes with extra small groups and individuals using the library media center—every day! The library media center, in fact, becomes an additional teaching space with flexible access, and it's okay for the library media specialist to not be the only teacher in the library media center. If she and others are teaching there, it means that the library media center is being used to capacity, and that is a real advantage.

Third, flexible access maximizes the use of the resources in the library media center. Perhaps the resources become slightly more worn because patrons check them out more often, but this is better than having books that sit on the shelves. If students are using the subscription databases all day, rather than just for an hour or two, the subscription certainly becomes more cost-effective. With flexible access, students, staff, and the rest of the school community can use the resources all the time.

Fourth, flexible access changes the way students are educated when the library media center becomes an annex to the classroom. Picture a classroom where teachers encourage the students to locate more resources through electronic technology. Picture a classroom where they are encouraged to go to the library media center to find out what they want to know. You have pictured encouragement of lifelong learning. Those students may go to the library media center as individuals, as small groups, or as whole classes. Creating lifelong learners, readers, and library users is a real advantage that comes with flexible access.

Fifth, flexible access encourages and helps patrons of the larger school community continue or become lifelong learners, readers, and library users when a school extends the library media center's services beyond its walls. Opening the library media center to the larger school community may provide those patrons with the only library at their disposal. Extending the services of the library media center can be a real advantage to the school community.

Sixth, patrons misplace or lose fewer library media center books when they can return and check out materials at any time. All library media specialists know how students check out a book in the morning, bring it back to the classroom, and then decide it isn't the right one. If they can return it right away, they will not lose or misplace the book. Allowing all-day checkout is another advantage of flexible access.

Seventh, flexible access promotes self-directed and self-paced learning. Students with the opportunity to use the library media center, its resources, and its services have the best chance of becoming lifelong learners, readers, and library users. There are many advantages to instituting flexible access in a library media center. After all, that's what we want—students who want to learn.

RECOGNIZING WHAT
FLEXIBLE SCHEDULING OFFERS

Flexible scheduling provides many advantages to a school because through flexible scheduling, teachers and the library media specialist can plan and provide timely and relevant library literacy lessons to students. Schools with flexible scheduling appreciate it and can see the advantages that occur when the library media specialist can turn the variables associated with it into noticeable advantages. Flexible scheduling, like flexible access, provides a positive thrust in a school community.

Facts and Figures Agree:
There Are Advantages to Flexible Scheduling

When students have more relevant library literacy lessons precisely when they need them, their projects and reports for the units of study will demonstrate that the students are accomplishing in-depth research. Members of the school's community, especially parents, will want the flexibly scheduled library literacy lessons to continue. The Library Power program, which required schools to keep and analyze data, generated information about flexible scheduling and school improvement plans. These facts and figures from *Lessons from Library Power* (Zweizig and McAfee Hopkins 1999) point to some of the advantages of flexible scheduling.

In the Library Power Schools where there is flexible access and flexible scheduling (Zweizig and McAfee Hopkins 1999, p. 50):

When library media specialists, principals, and teachers were asked if flexible scheduling *will* continue
        92.2% of the library media specialists said "yes"
        96.4% of the principals said "yes"
        93.1% of the teachers said "yes"

When library media specialists, principals, and teachers were asked if flexible access *should* continue
        98.2% of the library media specialists said "yes"
        97.8% of the principals said "yes"
        85.3% of the teachers said "yes"

Fig. 9.3. Facts and figures for flexible scheduling.

Figure 9.3 provides us with facts that support the flexible scheduling of classes. Library media specialists, principals, and teachers said flexible scheduling would continue; only the teachers gave a response of less than 90 percent in agreement; 85 percent agreed it should continue. The authors outlined various reasons for the teacher's lower percentages, citing that if they were not as involved with the program, they were not as supportive. The figures overwhelming supported the continuation of flexible scheduling once it has been implemented. Library media specialists and principals are sold on the idea of flexible scheduling. Perhaps the teachers did not see its advantages as the library media specialists and principals did. In Library Power schools, flexible scheduling is a "keeper."

Flexible scheduling encourages collaborative planning with teachers. The LRS Colorado study states, "When library media staff collaborate with classroom teachers, reading scores average increases of 8 percent or 18 to 21 percent" (Lance, Rodney, and Hamilton-Pennell 2000, p. 2). When the library media specialist collaborates with teachers to plan and teach library lessons that are precisely what the students need to accomplish classroom curriculum goals at a specific point in time, reading scores can increase as much as 21 percent. As mentioned before, a school that collaborates is a stronger school.

I rarely kept or looked at numbers regarding library media use at Waterloo Elementary School in Columbia, Maryland. I know I should have. When we wrote the school's improvement plan, I realized that we needed to measure the use of the library media center if we wanted to show that the concepts of flexible access and flexible scheduling helped reach our school goals. We stated in the plan that there would be a certain realistic percentage increase in the use of the library media center due to flexible access and scheduling, and there was. Each semester, there was a larger increase than expected. Part of the increase probably can be attributed to the increased focus on both flexible access and scheduling. Our school's overall test scores, which we also were targeting, showed an increase each year, too. Keeping track of the numbers is essential.

Linthicum Elementary School in Linthicum, Maryland, (Wilson 1993) kept track of how many hours of library media lessons each grade had first with a fixed schedule and then with a flexible schedule. On average, the classes had close to 20 percent more time in library media lessons than they did within a fixed schedule used the year before. The additional media library lessons outlined in Figure 4.15 indicate that each class can easily have six additional library media times during the year, with only minimal flexible scheduling. Having more library literacy lessons is an advantage.

Evelyn Conerly, the Library Power director in Baton Rouge, Louisiana, saw changes in all fifty-three of the schools that had Library Power funding for three years. She reported that "Teachers and librarians are working together as an instructional team and librarians are integrally involved in curriculum decisions. . . . The schools are using more trade books and fewer basal texts, and literature is being integrated into a variety of curriculum areas. . . . We've changed our way of doing things, and people seem to like it better" (Sadowski 1994, p. 31). Flexible scheduling changed the way the school was doing things, allowing library media specialists to become more actively involved with teachers and in the school. That's an advantage.

Some of the best facts to state the advantages of flexible scheduling are teachers' comments. Here are some comments from the teachers at Waterloo Elementary, which were gathered from a questionnaire distributed in March of 1994: "There's an opportunity for more in-depth study. The library has meaning rather than being just one more skill to learn. It creates interest and furthers opportunities to learn. It can cause conflicts with non-classroom teacher's schedules, yet that's a minor drawback which is definitely outweighed by the pluses." "I can see the most student achievement in the language arts lessons. I'd like to see more carryover into the other subject areas. Planning for the lessons is the part of flexible scheduling that is so difficult.

There never seems to be enough time or thought time available." And finally, "Coordination is time-consuming, yet flexible scheduling makes learning meaningful. It teaches children to apply what they learned. I see the most carryover when students can immediately use what they learned to create a finished project." These are honest comments that provided us with information from which to assess the success of flexible scheduling.

Usually, library media specialists and school districts that have implemented flexible scheduling do not want to go back to a fixed schedule. The gains made for everyone involved outweigh the adjustments and the changes that need to take place in a school when utilizing flexible scheduling. Most of all, flexible scheduling allows the library literacy lessons to be timely and relevant to create lifelong learners, reader, and library users. That is clearly an advantage.

There Are Additional Advantages to Flexible Scheduling

Of course, there are even more advantages to utilizing flexible scheduling for library media lessons. Chapters 2, 4, and 5 outlined the variables of flexible scheduling that I describe here as advantages. Some of these advantages are not self-evident, so they should be shared with the entire school community. The more they see them in action, the more a school community will welcome these advantages.

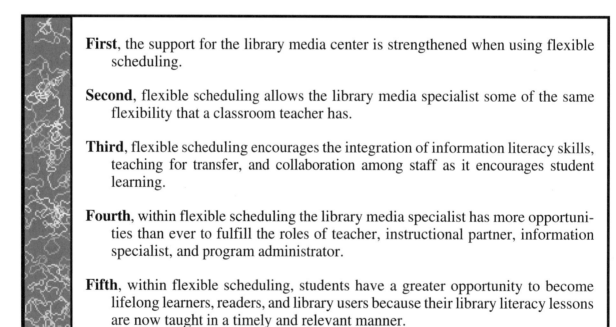

First, the support for the library media center is strengthened when using flexible scheduling.

Second, flexible scheduling allows the library media specialist some of the same flexibility that a classroom teacher has.

Third, flexible scheduling encourages the integration of information literacy skills, teaching for transfer, and collaboration among staff as it encourages student learning.

Fourth, within flexible scheduling the library media specialist has more opportunities than ever to fulfill the roles of teacher, instructional partner, information specialist, and program administrator.

Fifth, within flexible scheduling, students have a greater opportunity to become lifelong learners, readers, and library users because their library literacy lessons are now taught in a timely and relevant manner.

Fig. 9.4. Advantages to having flexible scheduling.

First, the support for the library media center is strengthened when utilizing flexible scheduling. When library media specialists teach library literacy lessons in response to an expressed need, the value is automatically increased in the eyes of the students, as well as the teachers. If students appreciate the library literacy lessons, their parents will as well. When teachers, staff, students, administrators, and parents see the results of the students learning more because library literacy lessons are timely and relevant, they will want flexible scheduling to continue. Of course, as with flexible access, when the school community sees that the library program has helped their students learn more, they generally will be more supportive of the library media program and the school.

Second, flexible scheduling allows the library media specialist some of the same flexibility that a classroom teacher has. The classroom teacher can break a class into groups for certain lessons or spend fifteen minutes on this and forty-five minutes on something else. The teacher also can extend a lesson to the next day and continue to build on the skills being taught. With flexible scheduling, the library media specialist can do the same thing with a library-literacy-related lesson. With a fixed schedule, the second grade's atlas-making lesson would have taken at least three weeks. With flexible scheduling, it was taught in two lessons scheduled three days apart (see Figure 2.4). In the library media center, as in the classroom, it is best to build on skills being taught in a timely fashion by offering flexibility to the teachers and the library media specialist.

Third, flexible scheduling encourages the integration of information literacy skills, teaching for transfer, and collaboration among staff as it encourages student learning. Although flexible scheduling is not necessary to facilitate any of those possibilities, it makes them more likely to occur because the library literacy lessons are taught in a more timely manner.

The teachers at Waterloo Elementary School, as noted earlier, commented on the way flexible scheduling was an advantage as related to the classroom curriculum. Flexible scheduling encourages the use of good teaching techniques and teaching content lesson at the point of need.

Fourth, with flexible scheduling, the library media specialist has more opportunities than ever to fulfill the roles of teacher, instructional partner, information specialist, and program administrator. Once teachers and the library media specialist start even casual planning and scheduling, the library media specialist can exercise these four potential roles of involvement in the school. By the time there's collaboration across the school, the library media specialist has become a part of every teaching team. She acts as an instructional partner when collaborating, gathers the necessary materials and technology, and manages the library media center in such a way that it will operate smoothly so that she can spend more time in the first three roles. In a school that has flexible scheduling, the library media specialist and the library media center become more responsive, supportive, and integral to the school's overall program and goals.

Fifth, with flexible scheduling, students have a greater opportunity to be come lifelong learners, readers, and library users because their library literacy lessons are taught in a timely and relevant manner.

OUTLINING THE ADDITIONAL ADVANTAGES TO FLEXIBLE ACCESS AND FLEXIBLE SCHEDULING TO THE SCHOOL COMMUNITY

Flexible access and flexible scheduling can be a catalyst for many things that strengthen a school and make its students more successful. Throughout this book, I have outlined and discussed the advantages of both flexible access and flexible scheduling. The following advantages may impact various members of the whole school community differently.

Following the suggestions in Chapter 6, the principal or the change agent would share with others the vision of the school's goal and how flexible access and flexible scheduling would facilitate that goal. The benefits of the changes that will occur as the school community works toward the school-wide goal need to be outlined, and support from the whole community needs to be gathered. Without community-wide support, the changes that are made will not be retained for any length of time. As the change agent presents the vision of the goal, everyone will draw their own conclusions and perhaps even have additional thoughts about the pros and cons of flexible access and scheduling. This is supposed to happen. As the school community, you can look at the possibilities and advantages and then decide what is doable and what is impossible for your school. The following are advantages of both flexible access and flexible scheduling that will benefit various members of the school community.

First, no matter what is the school's overall goal, flexible access and flexible scheduling will be in line with the goal and support it.

Second, the curriculum of a school benefits from additional input from the library media specialist, more resources from the library media center, and any level of coordination regarding the curriculum's content or teaching.

Third, working within flexible access and flexible scheduling can be just what is needed to continually keep a staff looking at how they teach and what they are teaching.

Fourth, flexible access and flexible scheduling increase the involvement of the library media specialist with the students and the school.

Fifth, with flexible access and flexible scheduling, the library media center becomes a wheel that drives a school to create lifelong learners, readers, and library users.

Fig. 9.5. Additional advantages of flexible access and flexible scheduling.

First, no matter what is the school's overall goal, flexible access and flexible scheduling will be in line with the goal and support it. As the brochure "The Principal's Manual for Your School Library Media Program" (American Association of School Librarians 2000) states, there are many great reasons for a principal and the school's administration to be interested and involved in the library media program. Overall, if a school is striving for academic achievement, instituting flexible access is a plus. In addition, with flexible access, the library media center is opened as an annex to the classroom. Using the library media center's resources will multiply the number of resources available to students. If a school is moving toward a resource-based curriculum, who better to have as part of the teaching team than the library media specialist who manages the library media center's resources and the library media center itself. If a school wants to integrate various skills into the classroom curriculum in a timely manner, utilizing flexible scheduling is an advantage and encourages collaboration among all staff members. In reality, any school-wide goal is encouraged, highlighted, and supported by the concepts of flexible access and flexible scheduling. Everyone benefits when a school seeks a school improvement goal, such as creating lifelong learners, readers, and library users. Everyone in the school community gains when a school is focused on attaining a goal that can be reached with the help of flexible access and flexible scheduling.

Second, the curriculum of a school benefits from additional input from the library media specialist, more resources from the library media center, and any level of coordination regarding the curriculum's content or teaching. A library media specialist gains an overview of the total school curriculum as she works and plans with the teachers. This is to everyone's advantage because with the library media specialist's knowledge of the curriculum can be streamlined, strengthened, organized, and adjusted to meet the needs of the students. If a school or district does not furnish a curriculum and the administration would like all the teachers in the same grade to teach the same units, implementing flexible access and flexible scheduling can be just the catalyst needed to create or fine tune any curriculum. As the curriculum falls into place, materials can be purchased to reflect the content of the curriculum, and the library media specialist can offer services that relate to it. Students, in particular, benefit when a school has a solid curriculum and the rest of the school community benefits when the students do.

Third, working within flexible access and flexible scheduling can be just what is needed to continually keep a staff looking at how they teach and what they are teaching. Some administrators and teachers will be uncomfortable with a schedule that isn't set, but there is an advantage to a flexible schedule. Flexible access and flexible scheduling allows the teachers and the library media specialist to be creative with their lessons. With flexible access, it is quite possible for the class to go to the library media center and research a topic, rather than just read about it in a book. With flexible scheduling, it is quite possible to have the library media specialist coteach the lessons and share the many resources of the library media center with the students. The library media specialist might even know of new print, nonprint, and electronic resources or teaching ideas that she can share with the teacher. Both flexible access and flexible scheduling can encourage a teacher to develop fresh ways to teach their curriculum, and this is an advantage for not only the teacher, but also the students, the administration, and the parents.

Fourth, flexible access and flexible scheduling increase the involvement of the library media specialist with the students and the school. If the library media specialist sees students two or three times a week as they come for a library literacy lesson or for other reasons such as checking out books, the library media specialist will begin to learn more about the students. She also will be working with the students around more productive and meaningful lessons. She increases her role in the school when she becomes part of the teaching teams. Perhaps when others see the library media specialist's involvement increasing with the students and staff, they might start increasing their own. The school community gains when the library media specialist and other staff members become stronger components in the school.

Fifth, with flexible access and flexible scheduling, the library media center becomes a wheel that drives a school to create lifelong learners, readers, and library users.

PRESENTING THE DISADVANTAGES AND MAKING ADJUSTMENTS AFTER FEEDBACK

The understanding and acceptance of and the support for flexible access and flexible scheduling will vary within school communities. In Chapter 6, Figure 6.2, I suggested that step five would be to include a presentation of the disadvantages of the changes and step six would provide opportunities for feedback. For changes to be lasting, these two steps are important. These steps show the school community that the leaders are realistic and truly want input about the vision of the school-wide goal.

Problems Are Possible

There are many possible problems related to flexible access and scheduling. Which problems will be hardest to overcome depends on the school. Some may find it difficult to accept the new role of the library media specialist; other schools may be frustrated with having a school schedule that doesn't include set library media times. Some schools may see many of the advantages I discussed as gains; others will see them as problems. The administrators of the school and the library media specialist are the ones who know which of the following items might be of concern to some or all of their staff:

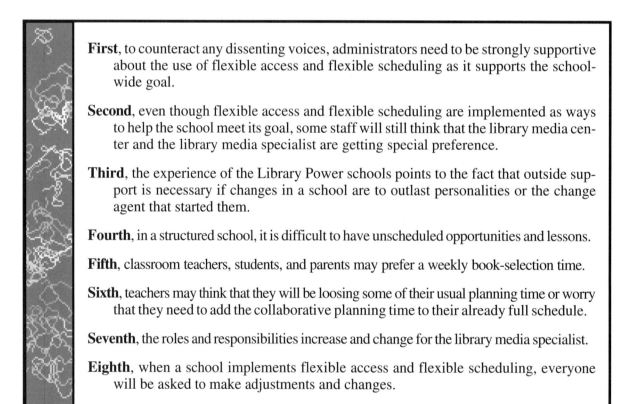

First, to counteract any dissenting voices, administrators need to be strongly supportive about the use of flexible access and flexible scheduling as it supports the school-wide goal.

Second, even though flexible access and flexible scheduling are implemented as ways to help the school meet its goal, some staff will still think that the library media center and the library media specialist are getting special preference.

Third, the experience of the Library Power schools points to the fact that outside support is necessary if changes in a school are to outlast personalities or the change agent that started them.

Fourth, in a structured school, it is difficult to have unscheduled opportunities and lessons.

Fifth, classroom teachers, students, and parents may prefer a weekly book-selection time.

Sixth, teachers may think that they will be loosing some of their usual planning time or worry that they need to add the collaborative planning time to their already full schedule.

Seventh, the roles and responsibilities increase and change for the library media specialist.

Eighth, when a school implements flexible access and flexible scheduling, everyone will be asked to make adjustments and changes.

Fig. 9.6. The disadvantages to the implementation of flexible access and flexible scheduling.

First, administrators need to be strongly supportive to counteract any dissenting voices about the use of flexible access and flexible scheduling as it supports the school-wide goal. The administrators may also need to direct funding for the library media center for new materials, staff development, and maybe even additional staffing rather than to other accounts. This action may not set well with the ones in charge of the other accounts. The administration can give support to a changing library media program by letting the school community know that adjustments can be made as the two concepts are implemented. Administrators will hear complaints, of course; and the hope is that there are not too many of them or that they come at the wrong time. Providing ways for the school community to give constructive feedback is important.

Second, even though flexible access and flexible scheduling are implemented as ways to help the school meet its goal, some staff will still think that the library media center and the library media specialist are getting special preference. There's always a line to walk to keep the focus on the ideas and concepts, not the person involved. It helps if the school library media center is referred to as "our" library media center so that everyone feels included in what is happening and gets some of the glory for the good results.

Third, the experience of the Library Power schools points to the fact that outside support is necessary if changes in a school are to outlast the personalities or the change agent that started them. That outside support comes from the community of the board of education staff members, government officials, businesses, and the general population. The support for flexible access and flexible scheduling needs to be broadened to include those outside the immediate walls of the school so that when key people inside the school leave, others will champion the concepts. Support from others outside the immediate school community also will strengthen the school and its lifelong learners, readers, and library users.

Fourth, in a structured school, it is difficult to have unscheduled opportunities and lessons. Staff, students, and parents expect everything to go according to a schedule. At a school like the Day School, students or whole classes may be at the library media center rather than in their room. Posting a copy of the library media center's and the library media specialist's schedule will put some fears to rest. Some people will get used to it over time and, as we know, others never will. Having some of the student's activities or classes off a fixed schedule can be unnerving to some.

Fifth, classroom teachers, students, and parents may prefer a weekly book-selection time. Some Library Power schools retained this, even though access to the library media center was flexible. Because most agree that students should come to the library media center at least once a week to check out materials, staff members will find a way to ensure that this happens. Older students can be held responsible to get to the library media center; adults in the school can encourage younger students to visit the library media center often. If your school prefers a regular book-selection time, perhaps you can institute this for the first quarter of the school year. As flexible access becomes more comfortable for all involved, students will come to the library media center two or three times a week, not just once a week.

Sixth, teachers may think that they will be loosing some of their usual planning time or worry that they need to add collaborative planning time to their already full schedule. In fact, normal teacher planning time gets moved around, but rarely lost. If teachers occasionally help with lessons in the library media center, their usual teacher planning time is still not reduced by much, and the rest of their usual planning time is just unscheduled. As a matter of fact, teachers generally get the same amount of planning time, if not more, with flexible scheduling; it's just that it's not always on the same day or at the same time. At first, more time is needed to bring the library media specialist on board with collaborative planning, and perhaps it is difficult to find a time when everyone can get together, but it gets easier. Teachers soon see that some of the planning and responsibilities that they had to do alone are now shared. It will take some time, but in the end, teachers will have as much planning time as they had in the past, as well as a partner to help teach their lessons. The library media specialist is the one who really adds to her planning time because she is now planning with all the staff, not just with herself. Planning and collaborating with others makes a school more cohesive.

Seventh, the roles and responsibilities increase and change for the library media specialist. When a school implements flexible access and flexible scheduling as ways to facilitate school-wide changes, the library media specialist needs to step forward and play a key role in the education of all students. Not only does the library media specialist have more responsibilities, but she is now assuming a leadership role in the school to promote the school improvement goal. Nonetheless, almost every library media specialist who has tried flexible access and flexible scheduling wouldn't go back to a fixed schedule in a million years.

Eighth, when a school implements flexible access and flexible scheduling, everyone will be asked to make adjustments and changes. Change is always a process and does not occur over night. Change is not a disadvantage when the school community sees the glass as half full.

As with any new idea, there are disadvantages to implementing flexible access and flexible scheduling. Nonetheless, the advantages listed in this chapter and elsewhere in the book clearly indicate that students will be more successful as lifelong learners, readers, and library users when schools allow them access to the library media center and teach timely and relevant library literacy lessons.

Adjustments Can Be Made Based on Feedback

Members of the school community should be given various opportunities to offer constructive feedback about the changes being implemented so that the school-wide goal can be met. Surveys, informal questionnaires, or direct questions for continuing evaluation can be used to bring out suggestions for improvement. Having a system for suggestions and feedback in place from the beginning is a wise move.

Once people give suggestions to the administrators, the library media specialist, and the library media technology committee, one or all of them may respond to the questionnaires with adjustments to be made or with additional explanation. For some involved with the changes, only one explanation is necessary; for others, weekly explanation and hand-holding may be in order. It is best to lay solid groundwork toward the acceptance of the implementation of the school-wide goal. You will build trust though the whole process, and that trust must be maintained. Most of the time feedback is valid, and many suggestions can help solve problems. Making adjustments based on feedback from the school community can be another positive step toward the goal of creating lifelong learners, readers, and library users.

CONTINUING TO OUTLINE THE ADVANTAGES OF FLEXIBLE ACCESS AND FLEXIBLE SCHEDULING

The advantages of flexible access and flexible scheduling need to be shared with the total school community when the concepts are introduced and again every month after that. Students, staff, teachers, parents, the board of education, businesses, government officials, and especially the administrators of the school need to hear and see the positive impact that flexible access and flexible scheduling have on the students' educational experiences. As the change team guiding the changes in the school, you can support the gathering of facts and figures or share in the telling of library success stories.

One can outline the advantages of flexible access and flexible scheduling in many ways. If your school is working within a school improvement plan, this is an excellent place to set numerical goals for flexible access and flexible scheduling. Publish facts, figures, and stories in newsletters, newspapers, and other media read by the members of the school community. Pictures of students coming into and using the library media center are truly worth a thousand words. Test scores can provide indicators that flexible access and flexible scheduling are positive. Seeking broad support for both flexible access and flexible scheduling is essential if they are to continue to benefit the students in a school. The immediate and wider school community needs to know the advantages associated with flexible access and flexible scheduling and how they create life-long learners, readers, and library users.

There are so many advantages to flexible access and flexible scheduling. Both concepts can be implemented in a variety of ways, but the results are harder to measure than the results of a standardized test. Logically, the advantages of having flexibility in the library media center outweigh the disadvantages. Allowing students the freedom to seek information when they need it and to be taught information when they can use it are advantages that lead to more advantages. The facts and figures show that flexible access and library media specialist collaboration with staff leads to an increase in the reading scores of the students. That is certainly an advantage.

Chapter 10

STEPPING FORWARD TO CREATE LIFELONG LEARNERS, READERS, AND LIBRARY USERS

Since Chapter 5, the team guiding the changes at the Afternoon School has been making progress toward their goal of becoming like the Day School. Their "shelves" are in order, and they are taking steps forward to create lifelong learners, readers, and library users. In that conference room, they're saying the following:

Okay, we're on our way to creating lifelong learners, readers, and library users. Yes we are. We've done a lot to become like the Day School.

I know we did a lot, but what exactly did we do?

Well, we started with preplanning and then convincing our administration that we wanted to make some changes in our school to change the way we educate our students.

I remember that, but then we started going forward in so many directions.

You're correct. As our "change team" grew, we were able to proceed with changes in many areas of our school. We made changes in our curriculum by streamlining it, as well as by streamlining the way we teach and the way the staff interacts with each other.

Our library media specialist has made a lot of changes, and the library media center is quite different now. It's great to have our library media specialist contributing so much to the school and to the students. It's also great to have so much community support for all we're doing.

Remember that flexible access to the library media center and the flexible scheduling of library literacy lessons has really improved our students' work.

Being prepared and understanding the change process helped us a lot, and I know having our principal so involved with the changes has really made a difference.

Well, the reason I asked, "exactly what did we do?" was because my friend at the Night School wanted to know how we've done it.

In case you, like the people at the Night School, are trying to figure out which foot to put forward down what path, let's discuss ways to take these steps forward and then highlight the paths to take to become like the Day School.

Fig. 10.1. The path to the Day School.

TAKING STEPS FORWARD

Each school situation is different; therefore, the way to take the steps to create lifelong learners, readers, and library users is different for each school. Flexibility is the key term in both flexible access and flexible scheduling. Everyone and everything around the two concepts should also be flexible. You can adjust, mold, manipulate, and create your own versions of flexible access, flexible scheduling, or both. Your situation will dictate how you and your school take the steps forward to create lifelong learners, readers, and library users.

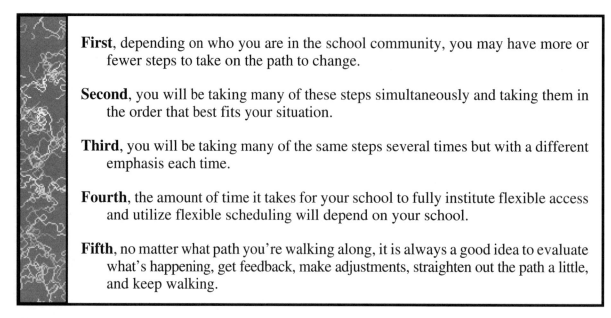

First, depending on who you are in the school community, you may have more or fewer steps to take on the path to change.

Second, you will be taking many of these steps simultaneously and taking them in the order that best fits your situation.

Third, you will be taking many of the same steps several times but with a different emphasis each time.

Fourth, the amount of time it takes for your school to fully institute flexible access and utilize flexible scheduling will depend on your school.

Fifth, no matter what path you're walking along, it is always a good idea to evaluate what's happening, get feedback, make adjustments, straighten out the path a little, and keep walking.

Fig. 10.2. Ways to take steps forward.

First, depending on who you are in the school community, you may have more or fewer steps to take on the path to change. If you are the school library media specialist, you have more steps to take than anyone else, and your first move after preplanning is to get the support of the school's administrators. If you are an administrator, yours is the most important role in terms of making the changes successful in your school. If you are a key teacher initiating changes at your school, you have both the library media specialist and administrative team to convince and to add to your "change team." If you are a school community member, you have the longest path to walk because you must convince the school staff to let you be the change agent. Each member of the team dealing with the changes in your school will fulfill a different role with regard to moving along the path to the end goal of creating lifelong learners, readers, and library users.

Second, you will be taking many of these steps simultaneously and taking them in the order that best fits your situation. Preplanning is always the first step, but after that you will most likely go on to step 2, 3, and 4 all in the same week. Because each school situation is different, it is up to you and others who are involved with the changes to decide where to put your energies and efforts. You might even be able to leave some steps out because your school is already walking on that path, or you might have to add steps to get started down a path. This process is not a one-step-at-a-time process; you take many steps at once.

Third, you will be taking many of the same steps several times but with a different emphasis each time. As a change agent introducing the idea of school-wide educational reform, you'll have to make a presentation to the administrators. Then there will be more presentations to the rest of the "change team" members as that team forms. Next comes the presentation to the school staff, then to the students and teachers, then the school community, and then to the business or local government communities as the years progress. You will give different presentations depending on the audience, and you will adjust these presentations many times. In a school setting, each year there will be new staff members and new school community members who must be brought on board. You will have to repeat certain steps you already have taken, although at different levels, if the change process is to keep moving along.

Fourth, the amount of time it takes for your school to fully institute flexible access and utilize flexible scheduling will depend on your school. There are those schools that set out a three-year plan, and those that prefer a five-year plan. This doesn't mean that you cannot start with both flexible access and flexible scheduling at the beginning of a new school year; it just means that implementing the concepts partially or fully will take time. Making lasting changes takes time.

Fifth, no matter what path you're walking along, it's always a good idea to evaluate what's happened, get feedback, make adjustments, straighten out the path a little, and then keep walking. Keeping a positive attitude and helping others to do the same, being reassuring to those who asked to make changes, and realigning the direction you're asking the school to go will keep the whole change process moving along as smoothly as it can.

TAKING THE PATHS TO CREATE LIFELONG LEARNERS, READERS, AND LIBRARY USERS

The Day School creates lifelong learners, readers, and library users because the total school community has accepted that outcome as its goal, and they work toward that goal every period of the day in every room of the school. Flexible access and flexible scheduling at the Day School library media center highlight, facilitate, and encourage what is happening in the rest of the school. There are many steps to take, seemingly all at once, to get started making the changeover to flexible access and or flexible scheduling in a school library media center. You, as a member of a team wishing to guide your school through these changes, have many responsibilities to accomplish. The library media specialist, in particular, has a number of responsibilities to meet. Let's outline the paths that branch off the many topics discussed in earlier chapters. These outlines will start your school, your school library media center, and your library media specialist on the path to flexible access and flexible scheduling that help, support, and encourage the creation of lifelong learners, readers, and library users in your school.

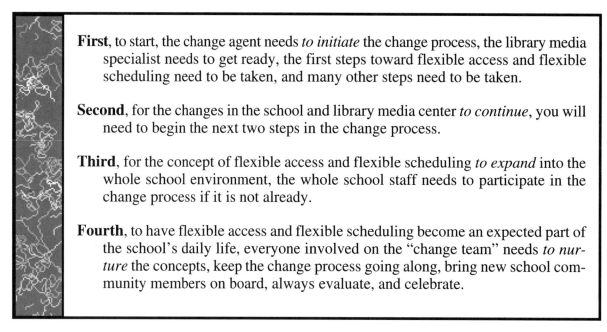

First, to start, the change agent needs *to initiate* the change process, the library media specialist needs to get ready, the first steps toward flexible access and flexible scheduling need to be taken, and many other steps need to be taken.

Second, for the changes in the school and library media center *to continue*, you will need to begin the next two steps in the change process.

Third, for the concept of flexible access and flexible scheduling *to expand* into the whole school environment, the whole school staff needs to participate in the change process if it is not already.

Fourth, to have flexible access and flexible scheduling become an expected part of the school's daily life, everyone involved on the "change team" needs *to nurture* the concepts, keep the change process going along, bring new school community members on board, always evaluate, and celebrate.

Fig. 10.3. The paths to flexible access and flexible scheduling.

       First, to start, the change agent needs *to initiate* the change process, the library media specialist needs to get ready, the first steps toward flexible access and flexible scheduling need to be taken, and many other steps need to be taken. Consider the following:

Everyone involved so far:

- The change agent needs to step forward as explained in Chapter 6.
- Reread Chapters 1 and 2 to refresh your understanding of flexible access and flexible scheduling.
- Convince the administrative team to make changes in the school and to implement flexible access and flexible scheduling using information in Chapter 9.
- Read some of the suggested readings listed in the bibliography.

- Reread the outline of the steps in the change process from Chapter 6 (Figure 6.2) and adjust them for your school.

- Initiate staff development for your library media specialist as mentioned in Chapters 3 and 6.

- Seek information and support from other schools, professional organizations, or others as discussed in Chapter 3.

The library media specialist:

- Reread "Preplanning" in Chapter 8.

- Start preplanning by making a school calendar and understanding the current school schedule.

- Convince the administrators about the benefits of flexible access and scheduling using the facts in Figures 9.1, 9.3, and in Chapter 9, remembering that Chapter 6 outlines how important the support of the principal is.

- Start setting up a plan book as described in Figures 5.7 and 5.8.

- Create a one-page listing of the information literacy skills as suggested in Figure 7.1.

- Start thinking about integrating some skills into the library literacy lessons as per the many examples in the book.

- Start planning with at least one teacher as discussed in Chapter 8.

- Double check the suggested changes from Chapter 3 to start preparing to add depth of the role of library media specialist (Figure 3.2) and assuming a leadership role (Figure 3.6) in the school.

Second, for the changes in the school and library media center *to continue*, you will need to begin the next two steps in the change process. The library media specialist and administrators can start seeking other supporters, the library media specialist can start instituting some flexible access and utilizing some flexible scheduling, and so on.

Everyone involved so far:

- The new vision needs to be presented and the steps to make changes outlined as noted in Chapter 6.

- Convince a few additional members of the school community to join the "change team" by sharing examples of flexible access and flexible scheduling from Chapters 4 and 5 and the figures in Chapter 9.

- Support the library media specialist as he starts to make changes and adjustments as listed in Chapter 3.

- See the library media specialist as a resource teacher, as mentioned in Chapter 3.

- Plan to make physical changes in the library media center and add more resources as the Library Power program did (Chapter 1).

- Streamline the school curriculum with the integration of skills in mind as described in Chapter 7.

- Start moving the school staff toward collaboration with some cooperation changing over to coordination as outlined in Chapter 8.

- Start collecting data that will be the baseline for your comparisons of before and after the changes were started.

- Provide staff development regarding flexible access and flexible scheduling for the "change team" and other key school community members.

- Seek out support for the changes being made from other schools or professional organizations as outlined in Chapter 6.

The library media specialist:

- Start assuming a leadership role in the school as outlined in Figure 3.6.

- Introduce some flexible access for student checkout and return and open the library media center to small groups and classes as described in Chapter 4 and outlined in Figures 4.2 and 4.3.

- Keep fine tuning the plan book.

- Start some flexible scheduling around orientation lessons, giving additional lessons, fifteen-minute lessons, or by taking advantage of the school's schedule as outlined in Chapter 4.

- Start changing over the management of the library media center by instituting a library media technology committee (Figure 3.3) and by increasing the number and responsibilities of volunteers (Figure 3.4) as outlined in Chapter 3.

- Reread the listing in Chapter 6 that outlines things the library media specialist can learn from others (Figure 6.3) and the areas where the library media specialist will need support (Figure 6.4).

- Integrate some information literacy skills into previously successful library media lessons (Chapter 7).

- Preplan first and then try planning and cooperating with a team on a unit of study as discussed in Chapter 8.

- Continue being involved in staff development opportunities and professional library organizations for support.

- Start giving in-services on various topics to the staff.

       Third, for the concept of flexible access and flexible scheduling *to expand* into the whole school environment, the whole school staff needs to participate in the change process if it is not already. The change process continues and the library media specialist moves toward fully implementing both flexible access and flexible scheduling.

Everyone involved so far:

- Share the school-wide goals with everyone in the school community, present the disadvantages, ask for feedback, and give the benefits of flexible access and flexible scheduling from your own newly collected information and figures and the information listed in Chapter 9.

- Support flexible access by encouraging its use and using it yourself.

- Support flexible scheduling by leading others to plan and schedule with the library media specialist as you do.

- Support the library media specialist's leadership role in the school and the changes he is making in the library media center.

- Add to the library media center budget for additional resources and staff when needed (Chapters 1 and 6).

- Initiate staff development for all in the immediate school community for them to learn more about integrating skills and collaboration.

- Seek support for your school from outside the immediate school community by informing the school district, businesses, and local governmental officials (Chapter 6).

- Keep on the lookout for additional books and articles that would be beneficial for your school community to read.

- Remain flexible as the change process continues.

- Keep taking data.

- Evaluate and celebrate. Many evaluation tools can be found, such as the ones in Epler 1999, Haycock 1999, Montana 1994, and Salomon 1996 (see Bibliography).

The library media specialist:

- Continue in a leadership role in the school as described in Chapter 3.

- Increase the amount of flexible access to the library media center (Chapter 5).

- Make the move to a blank planning book and utilize flexible scheduling when arranging all classes, even if some still fall at their old fixed times (Chapter 5).

- Integrate information literacy skills into the majority lessons.

- Maintain the professional connections and support that are in place.

- Continue with staff development.

- Continue to provide in-service opportunities to the staff.

- Continuing on the collaboration spectrum, move from coordinating to collaborate with most of the staff.

- Increase the involvement of the library media technology committee and volunteers in the management of the library media center.

Fourth, to have flexible access and flexible scheduling become an expected part of the school's daily life, everyone involved on the "change team" needs *to nurture* the concepts, keep the change process going along, bring new school community members on board, always evaluate, and celebrate.

Everyone involved so far:

- Keep the change process going, accept feedback, make adjustments, and be supportive of each other in the change process.
- Bring new students, parents, and school community members on board.
- Look for additional ways to maximize the students' learning experiences.
- Work collaboratively on all that is done in the school.
- Continually outline the advantages from Chapter 9 and add your own.
- Foster the community support already evident and seek out more.
- Remember that in-services and staff development are worthwhile and should be continued.
- Remain flexible as the change process continues.
- Keep taking data.
- Evaluate and celebrate.

The library media specialist:

- Maintain the leadership role.
- Continue adjusting flexible access and flexible scheduling to fit the students' and school's needs.
- Keep extending collaboration throughout the school.
- Recruit more volunteers and library media technology committee members to keep both situations fresh, as described in Chapter 3.
- Maintain a good amount of administrative time for managerial tasks (Chapter 5).
- Maintain professional ties and support.
- Always provide in-services for the staff.
- Start sharing the school's experiences with others.
- Evaluate and celebrate.

A school will set its own path toward its school-wide goals. Whether they want to be an Afternoon or a Day School, it is important to keep moving along the path to create lifelong learners, readers, and library users. You can use flexible access and flexible scheduling as a means of transporting your school to that goal. Flexible access to the library media center and flexible scheduling for library literacy lessons encourage schools to attain school-wide goals.

Students who have access to many varied library media resources and services in their school do become lifelong learners, readers, and library users. Students who are taught lessons integrating information literacy skills that fit with what they are learning in the classroom become lifelong learners, readers, and library users. If you teach students to locate for themselves the information and materials that they need, they will enjoy the lifelong gifts of learning, reading, and using the library.

If you, as a library media specialist, administrator, key teacher, or member of the school community are concerned with your students' educational experiences, you can support the changeover to flexible access to the library media center and the flexible scheduling for library literacy lessons. Implementing these and other changes will be the steps your school needs to take. Experience, facts, and figures all suggest that flexible access and flexible scheduling facilitate, encourage, and support the creation of lifelong learners, readers, and library users.

BIBLIOGRAPHY

American Association of School Librarians. 2000. *AASL Position Statement on Flexible Scheduling*. Available on the American Library Association Web site. URL: http://www.ala.org/aasl /positions/ps_flexible.html (accessed July 14, 2000).

American Association of School Librarians. 2000. *AASL Position Statement on Resource Based Instruction: Role of the School Library Media Specialist in Reading Development*. Available on the American Library Association Web site. URL: http://www.ala.org/aasl/positions /ps_reading.html (accessed July 14, 2000).

American Association of School Librarians. 2000. *AASL Position Statement on the Role of the School Library Media Program*. Available on the American Library Association Web site. URL: http://www.ala.org/aasl/positions/ps_roleschool.html (accessed July 14, 2000).

American Association of School Librarians. 2000. *AASL Position Statement on Information Literacy*. Available on the American Library Association Web site. URL: http://www.ala.org/aasl /positions/ps_infolit.html (accessed March 8, 2001).

American Association of School Librarians. 2000. *AASL Position Statements. American Library Association*. Available on the American Library Association Web site. URL: http://www.ala.org /aasl/positions/index.html (accessed July 14, 2000).

American Association of School Librarians. 2000. *Principal's Manual for Your School Library Media Program brochure*. Available on the American Library Association Web site. URL: http://www.ala.org/aasl/principalsmanual.html (accessed July 14, 2000).

American Library Association of School Librarians and Association for Educational Communications and Technology. 1998. *Information Power: Building Partnerships for Learning*. Chicago: American Library Association and Association for Educational Communications and Technology.

Bernstein, Allison. 1997. "Flexible Schedules: Quality Learning Time." *Library Talk* 10, no. 3 (May/June): 11.

Brown, Jean. 1999. "Changing Teaching Practice to Meet Current Expectation: Implications for Teacher-Librarians." In *Foundations for Effective School Library Media Programs*, edited by Ken Haycock, 175–81. Englewood, Colo.: Libraries Unlimited.

Brown, Jean. 1999. "Navigating the '90s—The Teacher-Librarian As Change Agent." In *Foundations for Effective School Library Media Programs*, edited by Ken Haycock, 65–72. Englewood, Colo.: Libraries Unlimited.

Browne, Karen Stevens. 1991. "Historical Fiction and Literature-Based Instruction." *School Library Media Activities Monthly* 7, no. 6 (February): 31–32+.

Browne, Karen Stevens. 1991. "Making the Move to Flexible Scheduling—Six Stepping Stones." *School Library Media Activities Monthly* 8, no. 1 (September): 28–29.

Browne, Karen Stevens, and Linda Burton. 1989. "Timing Is Everything: Adapting to the Flexible Schedule." *School Library Journal* 35 (December): 20–23.

Buchanan, Jan. 1991. *Flexible Access Library Media Programs*. Englewood, Colo.: Libraries Unlimited.

Coatney, Sharon. 1999. "President's Column: Good Teachers Teach." *Knowledge Quest* 27, no. 5 (May/June): 4.

Colorado Department of Education. 1999. *Colorado School Library Media Standards of Information Literacy and Competencies* (Draft). Denver, Colo.: Colorado Department of Education, Colorado Educational Media Association, Colorado State Library.

Dietz, Mary E. 1990. "On the Road to Change." *Instructor* (April): 35–37.

Donham van Deusen, Jean. 1999. "Prerequisites to Flexible Scheduling." In *Foundations for Effective School Library Media Programs*, edited by Ken Haycock, 223–27. Englewood, Colo.: Libraries Unlimited.

Donham van Deusen, Jean, and Julie I. Tallman. 1994. "The Impact of Scheduling on Curriculum Consultation and Information Skills Instruction: Part 1." *School Library Media Quarterly* (Fall): 17–25.

Epler, Doris. 1999. "Using Evaluation to Bring the School Library Resource Center Programs into Closer Alliance with *Information Power*." In *Foundations for Effective School Library Media Programs*, edited by Ken Haycock, 296–99. Englewood, Colo.: Libraries Unlimited.

"Focus on Flexible Scheduling." 1990. *School Library Media Quarterly* 19 (Fall): centerfold.

Fox, Carol J. "Flexible Scheduling—A Way to Integrate." Available on the Internet: URL: http://shoga.wwa.com/~cfox/alice/flex1.htm (accessed July 15, 2000).

Haycock, Ken. 1999. *Foundations for Effective School Library Media Programs*. Englewood, Colo.: Libraries Unlimited.

Haycock, Ken. 1999. "Evaluation of the Teacher Librarian: A Discussion Guide." In *Foundations for Effective School Library Media Programs*, edited by Ken Haycock, 305–11. Englewood, Colo.: Libraries Unlimited.

Haycock, Ken. 1999. "Research in Teacher Librarianship and the Institutionalization of Change." In *Foundations for Effective School Library Media Programs*, edited by Ken Haycock, 12–24. Englewood, Colo.: Libraries Unlimited.

Haycock, Ken, ed. 1999. *Media Programs*. Englewood, Colo: Libraries Unlimited.

Houff, Suzanne G. 1990. "Flexibility Is the Key." *School Library Media Activities Monthly* 7, no. 3 (November): 27.

Howard County Public School System. 1997. *Educational Technologies K–5: The Essential Curriculum Documents*, Ellicott City, Md.: Howard County Public School System.

Howard County Public School System. 1997. *Media K–5: The Essential Curriculum Documents*, Ellicott City, Md.: Howard County Public School System.

Hughes-Hassell, Sandra. 2001. "Implementing Change: What School Library Media Specialists Should Know." In *Knowledge Quest* 29, no. 3 (January/February): 11–15.

Ireland, LaVerne H. 1993. *The Impact of School Library Services on Student Academic Achievement—An Annotated Bibliography*. 3d ed. Morgan Hill, Calif.: Petervin Press.

Jay, M. Ellen. 1989. "Flexible Scheduling: Potential for Impact." In *School Library Media Annual 1989 Volume Seven*, edited by Jane Bandy Smith, 57–60. Englewood, Colo.: Libraries Unlimited.

Jay, M. Ellen, and Hilda L. Jay. 1994. "The Changed Role of the Elementary Library Media Teacher." *The Reference Librarian* 44: 61–69.

Johnson, Doug. 1997. *The Indispensable Librarian: Surviving (and Thriving) in School Media Centers*. Worthington, Ohio: Linworth Publishing.

Johnson, Doug. 2000. "The New Improved School Library." Presented at a concurrent session, Colorado Educational Media Association Conference, Colorado Springs, Colo., Februrary 18, 2000. Available on the Internet: URL: http://doug-johnson.com/pres.html (accessed July 15, 2000).

Johnson, Doug. 1999. "Why Do Libraries Need All Those Support People?" *Knowledge Quest* 27, no. 4 (March/April): 43–44.

Kansas Association of School Librarians. 1999. "Planning and Assessing Learning Across the Curriculum." *Knowledge Quest* 28, no. 1 (September/October): 10–16.

Krimmelbein, Cindy Jeffrey. 1989. *The Choice to Change*. Englewood, Colo.: Libraries Unlimited.

Lance, Keith Curry. 2000. "Information Empowering: How School Librarians Help Kids Achieve Standards." Presented at a concurrent session, Colorado Educational Media Association Conference, Colorado Springs, Colo., February 19, 2000.

Lance, Keith Curry. 1994. "The Impact of School Library Media Centers on Academic Achievement." *School Library Media Quarterly* (Spring): 167–72.

Lance, Keith Curry. 1992. *The Impact of School Library Media Centers on Academic Achievement*. Denver, Colo.: Colorado Department of Education.

Lance, Keith Curry, Marcia J. Rodney, and Christine Hamilton-Pennell. 2000. "How School Librarians Help Kids Achieve Standards: The Second Colorado Study." Available on the Library Research Service Web site: URL: http://www.lrs.org/pdf/lmc/CO2brochure.pdf (accessed August 17, 2000).

Lankford, Mary K. 1994. "Flexible Access." *School Library Journal* 40, no. 8 (August): 21–23.

Library Research Service. *Internet, Fast Facts No. 164—November 19, 1999, Proof of the Power: A First Look at the Results of the Colorado Study . . . and More!* Available on the Library Research Service Web site: URL: http://www.lrs.org/html/school_studies.html (accessed August 16, 2000).

Loertscher, David V. 1988. *Taxonomies of the School Library Media Program*. Englewood, Colo.: Libraries Unlimited.

Miller, Donna P., and J'Lynn Anderson. 1996. *Developing an Integrated Library Program*. Worthington, Ohio: Linworth Publishing.

Montana Office of Public Instruction. 1994. *Montana Library and Information Skills Model Curriculum*. Helena, Mont.: Office of Public Instruction.

Ohlrich, Karen Browne. 1996. "What Are We? Library Media Information Specialists, Computer, Technology Coordinators, Teachers Instructional Consultants, School-Base Management Team Members, or What?" *School Library Media Activities Monthly* 12, no. 9 (May): 26–28.

Ohlrich, Karen Browne. 1992. "Flexible Scheduling: The Dream vs. Reality." *School Library Journal* 38, no. 5 (May): 35–38.

Oswald, Marilyn K. 1994. "Implementing and Maintaining Successful Flexible Scheduling in Elementary School Library Media Programs."(Master of Science report, Minnesota State University, Mankato, Minn.).

Page, Carol-Ann. 1999. "Collaborative Planning: A Model That Works." In *Foundations for Effective School Library Media Programs*, edited by Ken Haycock, 189–204. Englewood, Colo: Libraries Unlimited.

Pickard, Patricia W. 1994. "The Instructional Consultant Role of the Library Media Specialist: A Progress Report," *School Library Activities Monthly* 10, no. 5 (January): 27–29.

Putman, Eleanor. 1996. "The Instructional Consultant Role of the Elementary-School Library Media Specialist and the Effects of Program Scheduling on Its Practice." *School Library Media Quarterly* 25, no. 1 (Fall): 43–49.

Rowling, J. K. 1998. *Harry Potter and the Chamber of Secrets*. New York, N.Y.: Scholastic Press.

Sadowski, Michael. 1994. "The Power to Grow: Success Stories from the National Library Program." *School Library Journal* 40, no. 7 (July): 30–35.

Salmon, Sheila, Elizabeth K. Goldfarb, Melinda Greenblatt, and Anita Phillips Strauss. 1996. *Power Up Your Library: Creating the New Elementary School Library Program.* Englewood, Colo.: Libraries Unlimited.

Sparks, Linda R., and Barbara Sorrow. 1991. *Teachers and Librarians Working Together: To Make Students Lifelong Library Users.* Jefferson, N.C.: McFarland & Company.

Straathof, Sharon. 1999. Developing a School-Based Research Strategy K–7. In *Foundations for Effective School Library Media Programs*, edited by Ken Haycock, 130–39. Englewood, Colo.: Libraries Unlimited.

Tallman, Julie I., and Jean Donham van Deusen. 1995. "Is Flexible Scheduling Always the Answer? Some Surprising Results from a National Study." In *School Library Media Annual, 1995*, 201–5. Englewood, Colo.: Libraries Unlimited.

Tallman, Julie I., and Jean Donham van Deusen. 1994. "External Conditions As They Relate to Curriculum Consultation and Information Skills Instruction by School Library Media Specialists: Part 2." *School Library Media Quarterly* (Fall): 24–31.

Tallman, Julie I., and Jean Donham van Deusen. 1994. "Collaborative Unit Planning—Schedule, Time, and Participants: Part 3." *School Library Media Quarterly* (Fall): 33–37.

Teger, Nancy L., and Donna Nunn. 1999. "Impact of Block Schedules on Library Media Centers." *Knowledge Quest* 28, no. 2 (November/December): 10–15.

Turner, Philip M. 1993. *Helping Teachers Teach.* Englewood, Colo.: Libraries Unlimited.

Vanek, Doris. 1994. "The Challenge to Change: Dealing with Resistant, Entrenched, and Uncooperative Foot Dragger." *Center Page* (Winter): 1. Columbia, Md.: Howard County Public School System.

Wilson, Bonnie. 1993. "Linthicum Elementary School Flexible Access Program Review." Handout from Linthicum Elementary School, 101 School Lane, Linthicum, MD 21090.

Wolcott, Linda Lachance. 1994. "Understanding How Teachers Plan: Strategies for Successful Instructional Partnerships." *School Library Media Quarterly* (Spring): 161–64.

Woolls, Blanche. 1999. *The School Library Media Manager*, 2d ed. Englewood, Colo.: Libraries Unlimited.

Zweizig, Doulgas L., and Dianne McAfee Hopkins. 1999. *Lessons from Library Power: Enriching Teaching and Learning.* Englewood, Colo.: Libraries Unlimited.

INDEX

Media Center Must-Haves

from *Libraries Unlimited*

100 MOST POPULAR SCIENTISTS FOR YOUNG ADULTS
Biographical Sketches and Professional Paths
Kendall Haven and Donna Clark

Revealing the career histories of successful 20th Century scientists, this exciting resource offers students a wonderful research tool and words of advice from great scientists on launching a science career. Much more than a collection of biographies, this is an inspiring and practical tool for students interested in science careers. **Grades 7–12.**
Profiles and Pathways Series
xv, 525p. 7x10 cloth ISBN 1-56308-674-3

BULLETIN BOARDS AND 3-D SHOWCASES THAT CAPTURE THEM
WITH PIZZAZZ
Karen Hawthorne and Jane E. Gibson

This illustrated how-to guide provides detailed instructions, supply lists, and variations for an entire year (including summers and holidays) of exciting displays. Easily adapted to any subject or budget, these bulletin boards and showcases—proven favorites for students in middle and high school—will also excite the imaginations of younger students. **Grades 5–12.**
ix, 147p. 8½x11 paper ISBN 1-56308-695-6

GOTCHA!
Nonfiction Booktalks to Get Kids Excited About Reading
Kathleen A. Baxter and Marcia Agness Kochel

Booktalks and support materials for more than 350 nonfiction titles are organized according to topics popular with young readers: "Great Disasters," "Unsolved Mysteries," "Fascinating People," "Science," and "Fun Experiments To Do." These concrete, classroom-tested ideas help you effortlessly present the best of children's literature in irresistible ways. **Grades 1–8.**
xviii, 183p. 8½x11 paper ISBN 1-56308-683-2

THE INTERNET RESOURCE DIRECTORY FOR K–12 TEACHERS
AND LIBRARIANS
Elizabeth B. Miller

With its curriculum-driven organization, simple instructions, and a wealth of information, this guide is simply the best Internet directory available for educators. All previous site annotations are updated as needed, and double-checked for accuracy. **All Levels.**
*Call for information on most recent edition.

STUDENT CHEATING AND PLAGIARISM IN THE INTERNET ERA
A Wake-Up Call
Ann Lathrop and Kathleen Foss

Put a stop to high-tech and more traditional low-tech forms of cheating and plagiarism. Also, learn to recognize the danger signs for cheating and how to identify material that has been copied. Sample policies for developing academic integrity, reproducible lessons for students and faculty, and lists of helpful online and print resources are included. A must-read for concerned educators, administrators, and parents. **Grades 4–12.**
xiv, 255p. 6x9 paper ISBN 1-56308-841-X

For a free catalog or to place an order, please contact:
Libraries Unlimited
88 Post Road West • P.O. Box 5007 • Westport • CT 06881
Phone: 800-225-5800 • Fax: 203-750-9790
Web site: www.lu.com